Kids' Knits
for Heads, Hands & Toes

Kids' Knits
for
Heads, Hands & Toes

More than 40
original patterns
for 0-7 year olds

Debbie Bliss

St. Martin's Griffin

New York

This book is dedicated to Barry, Billy and Eleanor:

Library of Congress Cataloging-in-Publication Data

Bliss, Debbie
    Kids' Knits for heads, hands, and toes/Debbie Bliss
        p.   cn.
    ISBN 0-812-08038-7
      1. Knitting--Patterns.   2. Children's clothing.   I. Title
  TT825.B563 1992
  746,9'2--dd20

First St. Martin's Griffin Edition/1996
10 9 8 7 6 5 4 3 2 1

Published in Great Britain by Ebury Press

Photography by Sandra Lousada
Designed by Jerry Goldie
Styling by Marie Willey

Typeset by Textype Typesetters, Cambridge
Printed and bound in Italy by New Interlitho,
S.p.a., Milan

Also by Debbie Bliss
Baby Knits
New Baby Knits
Kids' Country Knits
Toy Knits
Debbie Bliss Nursery Knits

The author and publishers would like to thank the following for lending clothes for photography.

General Clothing Co., The Camberwell Business Centre,
    99–103 Lomond Grove, London SE5. Tel 071 703 1974
The Nursery, 03 Bishops Road, London SW6
    Tel 071 731 6637
Nipper Mail Order, Gloucester House, 45 Gloucester Street,
    Brighton, East Sussex. Tel 0273 693785
Jacardi, 473 Oxford Street, London W1. Tel 071 491 9141
Next Boys and Girls, Kensington High Street, London W8.
Hennes, 276 Regent Street, London W1 and branches.
Scotch House, 2 Brompton Road, London SW1.
Bananas, 46 Bourne Street, London SW1.
Trotters, 34 King's Road, London SW3.
Jones the Bookmakers – branches nationwide.
Jeffrey Rogers Juniors. Tel 071 631 4142
GEO Trowark 17 St Christopher's Place, London W1.

Contents

Introduction

As the mother of young children, I know they love any opportunity to dress up. With this in mind, my aim in this book has been to design knits that are not only practical and comfortable, but which children will also find stylish and fun to wear.

There are over 40 patterns here, including winter outfits of hats, scarves, mittens and socks and ethnic-inspired cotton caps for summer. The designs range from classic berets and shawls to fun animal hats and bootees for babies. All the yarns used are machine-washable. Many of the garments can be knitted with oddments of yarn and are quick and easy to knit. Knitting smaller items can be very enjoyable and in my experience it's an excellent way for new or young knitters to build up their confidence, creating something with an individual, hand-crafted look in the process.

Author's Acknowledgments

I would like to thank the following for their generous help: Gisela Blum for her practical and technical assistance, Berenice Goodchild, Kate Jones, Milly Johnson, and once again, Fiona McTague for her practical and moral support, and for contributing the "Birds" Hat and Bag, and the swatch for the Fair Isle Shawl.

I am grateful for the invaluable help of the following knitters: Lynda Clarke, Isobel Kemp, Miriam Hudson, Sylvia Stevens, Frances Wallace, Betty Webb.

I would also like to thank Tina Egleton for her technical expertise and pattern checking, Sandra Lousada for the beautiful photography, Marie Willey for perfect styling, Denise Bates for her support, and Fiona MacIntyre and Heather Jeeves for making the book possible.

Debbie Bliss

Striped "Wee Willie Winkie" Hat and Socks and Teddy Bear

SEE PAGE
42

Teddy Bear Hood,
Mittens and Bootees
SEE PAGE
43

Duck Hood and Bootees
SEE PAGE
44

Mouse Hat and Bootees
SEE PAGE
45

Multi-coloured Hat and
Socks
SEE PAGE
46

Crown Hat
SEE PAGE
47

Nursery Hat and Shoes
SEE PAGE
48

Christmas Pudding Hat and Mittens
SEE PAGE
49

Mexican Poncho with Pompons and Hat
SEE PAGE
50

Inca Hat and Socks
SEE PAGE
51

Ladybird Hat and Slippers
SEE PAGE
52

Reindeer Hat, Scarf,
Mittens and Socks
SEE PAGE
53

Christmas Tree Hat
SEE PAGE
56

Jester Hat and Gloves
SEE PAGE
56

Segment Hat
SEE PAGE
57

Clown Hat, Mittens and
Slippers
SEE PAGE
58

*Floppy Velvet Hat and
Velvet Hat*
SEE PAGE
59

Crochet Bonnet and Lace-trimmed Hat
SEE PAGE
60

Elephant Hat and Mittens
SEE PAGE
61

Plain "Wee Willie Winkie" Hat, Mittens and Slippers
SEE PAGE
62

African-style Hat
SEE PAGE
63

Toy Hat
SEE PAGE
64

Peruvian Hat and Socks and Mexican Dolls
SEE PAGES
65–66

Plain Fur-lined Hat and
Fur-lined Fair Isle Hat
SEE PAGES
68–69

Aran Hats
SEE PAGE
67

*Aran Scarf and
Fingerless Gloves*
SEE PAGE
70

*Fair Isle Triangle Scarf,
Gloves and Socks*
SEE PAGE
71

Tweedy Hat and Mittens
SEE PAGE
73

Striped Beret, Scarf and Gloves
SEE PAGE
75

Diamond Pattern
Crochet Hat and Striped
Crochet Hat
SEE PAGE
74

Fair Isle Beret and Gloves
SEE PAGE
76

"Birds" Hat and Bag
SEE PAGE
77

*Two-colour Beret,
Gloves and Socks*
SEE PAGE
78

*Fair Isle Ski Hat and
Generous Mittens*
SEE PAGE
79

The Patterns

BASIC INFORMATION

ABBREVIATIONS

alt-alternate, **beg**-begin(ning), **cm**-centimetres, **cont**-continue, **dec**-decreas(e)ing, **foll**-following, **g**-gramme, **inc**-increas(e)ing, **in**-inch(es), **K**-knit, **m1**-make one by picking up loop lying between st just worked and next st and work into the back of it, **mm**-millimetre, **patt**-pattern, **P**-purl, **psso**-pass slipped stitch over, **rem**-remain(ing), **rep**-repeat, **sl**-slip, **st**-stitch, **st st**-stocking stitch, **tbl**-through back of loops, **tog**-together, **yb**-yarn back, **yf**-yarn forward, **yon**-yarn over needle, **yrn**-yarn round needle.

NOTES

Figures for larger sizes are given in ( ) brackets. Where only one figure appears, this applies to all sizes.

Work figures given in [ ] the number of times stated afterwards.

Where 0 appears no stitches or rows are worked for this size.

YARNS

All amounts are based on average requirements and should therefore be regarded as approximate. Use only the yarn specified if possible.

If, however, you cannot find the actual yarn specified, you can substitute a yarn of similar weight. Make sure that the substituted yarn knits up to the tension specified in the instructions (see below).

TENSION

Each pattern in this book specifies tension – the number of stitches and rows per centimetre (inch) that should be obtained on given needles, yarn and stitch pattern. Check your tension carefully before commencing work.

Use the same yarn, needles and stitch pattern as those to be used for main work and knit a sample at least 12.5x12.5 cm (5 in) square. Smooth out the finished sample on a flat surface but do not stretch it. To check the tension place a ruler horizontally on the sample and mark 10 cm (4 in) across with pins. Count the number of stitches between pins. To check the row tension place ruler vertically on sample and mark out 10 cm (4 in) with pins. Count the number of rows between pins. If the number of stitches and rows is greater than specified try again using larger needles; if less use smaller needles.

The stitch tension is the most important element to get right.

CIRCULAR KNITTING

Some of the garments in this book have been knitted in the round on double pointed needles. Circular or tubular knitting is worked in continuous rounds to make a seamless fabric.

There are a few important points to remember:

1. The bottom edge of all stitches must face the centre, thus avoiding twisting the work.
2. A marker such as a length of coloured thread should be placed at the end of the cast on edge to indicate the end of rounds, and moved up as the work progresses.
3. Yarn must be pulled firmly when knitting the first stitch on each of the double pointed needles, to avoid a ladder effect.

When working with a set of double pointed needles: Divide the number of stitches to be worked on or cast on between three needles, leaving one needle free for working with. Lay the three needles in a triangle. With fourth (working) needle, join work by working into first cast on stitch on first needle, pulling the yarn tightly to avoid a gap. Knit all stitches on first needle, and using this needle as a working needle, knit stitches on second and third needles as before. Slip marker and begin next round.

Striped "Wee Willie Winkie" Hat and Socks

See Page
7

MATERIALS

Hat 1×50g ball of Hayfield Raw Cotton Classics 4 ply in each of Black (A) and Cream (B).
Set of four in each of 2¾mm (No 12/US 1) and 3¼mm (No 10/US 3) double-pointed knitting needles.
Socks Small amount of Hayfield Raw Cotton Classics 4 ply in each of Black (A) and Cream (B).
Set of four in each of 2¾mm (No 12/US 1) and 3mm (No 11/US 2) double-pointed knitting needles.

MEASUREMENTS

To fit age
3(6: 9) months

TENSION

28 sts and 36 rows to 10cm/4in square over st st on 3¼mm (No 10/US 3) needles.
30 sts and 38 rows to 10cm/4in square over st st on 3mm (No 11/US 2) needles.

ABBREVIATIONS

See page 41.

Hat

With set of four 2¾mm (No 12/US 1) needles and A, cast on 104(114:122) sts.
Place marker after last st to indicate end of rounds. Taking care not to twist the work, cont in rounds of K1, P1 rib for 3cm/1¼in.
Dec round *Rib 4(3: 1), [work 2 tog, rib 2(2: 3), work 2 tog, rib 2(3: 3)] 6 times; rep from * once. 80(90: 98) sts.
Change to set of four 3¼mm (No 10/US 3) needles.
Working in rounds of st st (every round K) and stripe patt of 4 rounds B and 2 rounds A throughout, cont until work measures 14(16: 18)cm/5½(6¼:7)in from beg, dec 2 sts evenly across last round on 2nd and 3rd sizes only. 80(88: 96) sts.
Shape top
Dec round [K18(20: 22), K2 tog] 4 times. Work 3 rounds.
Dec round [K17(19: 21), K2 tog] 4 times. Work 3 rounds.
Dec round [K16(18: 20), K2 tog] 4 times. Cont in this way, dec 4 sts as set on every 4th round until 8 sts rem.
Dec round [K2 tog] 4 times.
Break off yarn, thread end through rem sts, pull up and secure. Join seam. With A, make a large pompon and attach to top.

Socks

With set of four 2¾mm (No 12/US 1) needles and A, cast on 30(36: 40) sts.
Place marker after last st to indicate end of rounds. Taking care not to twist the work, cont in rounds of K1, P1 rib for 8 rounds.
Change to set of four 3mm (No 11/US 2) needles.
Working in rounds of st st (every round K) and stripe patt of 4 rounds B and 2 rounds A throughout, patt 18(24: 30) rounds. Break off yarns.
Shape heel
Slip last 7(9: 10) sts of last round and first 8(9: 10) sts of next round onto one needle for heel, divide rem 15(18: 20) instep sts onto two needles.
With right side facing rejoin B yarn to 15(18: 20) heel sts. Beg with a K row and working in st st and stripe patt of 4 rows B and 2 rows A, work 14(16: 16) rows.
Cont in B only.
Next row K9(10: 12), K2 tog tbl, K1, turn.
Next row Sl 1 purlwise, P4(3: 5), P2 tog, P1, turn.
Next row Sl 1 knitwise, K5(4: 6), K2 tog tbl, K1, turn.
Next row Sl 1 purlwise, P6(5: 7), P2 tog, P1, turn.
2nd and 3rd sizes only
Next row Sl 1 knitwise, K(6: 8), K2 tog tbl, K1, turn.
Next row Sl 1 purlwise, P(7: 9), P2 tog, P1, turn.
All sizes
Next row Sl 1 knitwise, K7(8: 10), K2 tog tbl, turn.
Next row Sl 1 purlwise, P7(8: 10), P2 tog. 9(10: 12) sts.
Break off yarn.
Shape instep
Next round Slip first 4(5: 6) heel sts onto a safety pin, rejoin B yarn to rem heel sts, K5(5: 6), pick up and K8(9: 9) sts along side edge of heel, K15(18: 20) instep sts, pick up and K8(9: 9) sts along other side edge of heel, K4(5: 6) sts from safety pin. 40(46: 50) sts.
Keeping stripe patt correct, work as follows:
Dec round K11(12: 13), K2 tog, K15(18: 20), K2 tog tbl, K10(12: 13).
K 1 round.
Dec round K10(11: 12), K2 tog, K15(18: 20), K2 tog tbl, K9(11: 12).
K 1 round.
Dec round K9(10: 11), K2 tog, K15(18: 20), K2 tog tbl, K8(10: 11).
Cont in this way, dec 2 sts as set on every alt round until 30(34: 38) sts rem. Patt 10(14: 18) rounds straight.
Shape toes
Dec round [K5(6: 7), K2 tog, K2, K2 tog tbl, K4(5: 6)] twice.
K 1 round.
Dec round [K4(5: 6), K2 tog, K2, K2 tog tbl, K3(4: 5)] twice.
K 1 round.
Dec round [K3(4: 5), K2 tog, K2, K2 tog tbl, K2(3: 4)] twice.
Cont in this way, dec 4 sts as set on every alt round until 14 sts rem.
K 1 round.
Dec round [K1, K2 tog, K2, K2 tog tbl] twice.
Dec round Sl 2, K2, sl 1, K2 tog, psso, K2, sl 1, K2 tog the 2 slipped sts from beg of round, psso.
Break off yarn, thread end through rem sts, pull up and secure.

Teddy Bear

See Page
7

MATERIALS

1×50g ball of Hayfield Grampian DK in main colour (MC).
Oddment of Black for embroidery.
Pair of 3¼mm (No 10/US 3) knitting needles.
Small amount of wadding.

MEASUREMENTS

Approximately 16cm/6½in high.

ABBREVIATIONS

See page 41.

Body

Begin at lower edge.
With 3¼mm (No 10/US 3) needles and MC, cast on 14 sts.
Inc row K1, [K twice in next st] 12 times, K1. 26 sts.
Beg with a P row, work 3 rows in st st.
Inc row K7, m1, K11, m1, K8.
Work 5 rows in st st.
Inc row K7, m1, K13, m1, K8.

Work 6 rows in st st.
Dec row P7, P2 tog, P13, P2 tog, P6.
Work 2 rows in st st.
Dec row [K2 tog] to end.
Dec row [P2 tog] to end. 7 sts.
Break off yarn, thread end through rem
sts, pull up and secure.

Legs (make 2)
Begin at sole.
With 3¼mm (No 10/US 3) needles and
MC, cast on 10 sts.
Inc row K1, [K twice in next st] 8 times,
K1. 18 sts.
Beg with a P row, work 3 rows in st st.
Dec row K4, K2 tog, [K3 tog] twice, K2
tog, K4.
Work 9 rows in st st, inc one st at each
end of 2nd row. 14 sts.
Dec row [K2 tog] to end. 7 sts.
P 1 row. Break off yarn, thread end
through rem sts, pull up and secure.

Arms (make 2)
Begin at top.
With 3¼mm (No 10/US 3) needles and
MC, cast on 7 sts.
Inc row K1, [K twice in next st] 5 times,
K1. 12 sts.

Beg with a P row, work 9 rows in st st.
Dec row K3, [K2 tog] 3 times, K3.
Work 3 rows in st st.
Dec row K1, [K2 tog] to end. 5 sts.
Break off yarn, thread end through rem
sts, pull up and secure.

Head
Begin at centre back.
With 3¼mm (No 10/US 3) needles and
MC, cast on 12 sts. K 1 row.
Inc row P1, [P twice in next st] 10 times,
P 1. 22 sts.
Beg with a K row, work 4 rows in st st.
Inc row K6, m1, K1, m1, K8, m1, K1, m1,
K6.
Work 3 rows in st st.
Inc row K7, m1, K1, m1, K10, m1, K1,
m1, K7.
P 1 row.
Dec row K1, [K2 tog] to last st, K1.
P 1 row.
Dec row K2 tog, K3, [K3 tog] twice, K3,
K2 tog.
P 1 row.
Dec row [K2 tog] to end. 5 sts.
Break off yarn, thread end through rem
sts, pull up and secure.

Ears (make 2)
With 3¼mm (No 10/US 3) needles and
MC, cast on 8 sts.
Cont in st st, work 2 rows. Dec one st at
each end of next 2 rows. Inc one st at
each end of next 2 rows. Work 2 rows.
Cast off.

To Make Up
Join back seam of body and legs,
underarm seam of arms and bottom seam
of head, leaving cast on edges free. Stuff,
then run a gathering thread round cast on
edges, pull up and secure. With sewing
needle, attach yarn to inner edge of top of
one leg, then pass needle through body
at side approximately 1cm/¼in from base,
catch inner edge of top of other leg, then
pass needle through body again in same
place and catch inner edge of first leg
again in same place, pull yarn tightly to
depress legs and fasten off securely.
Attach arms to top of body in same way.
Fold ears in half widthwise and join seam
all round. Sew ears in position. With
Black, embroider face, then sew head to
body.

Teddy Bear Hood, Mittens and Bootees

See Page
8

MATERIALS
Hood 1×50g ball of Hayfield Pure
Wool Classics DK or Hayfield
Grampian DK in main colour (MC).
Small amount of same in contrast
colour (A). 1 button.
Small amount of wadding.
Mittens and Bootees 1×50g ball of
Hayfield Pure Wool Classics DK or
Hayfield Grampian DK in main colour
(MC).
Small amount of same in contrast
colour (A).
Pair each of 3¼mm (No 10/US 3) and
4mm (No 8/US 5) knitting needles.

MEASUREMENTS
Hood To fit age
3–6 (6–9) months
Mittens and Bootees To fit age
3–9 months

TENSION
22 sts and 28 rows to 10cm/4in
square over st st on 4mm (No 8/US
5) needles.

ABBREVIATIONS
See page 41.

Hood

Main part
With 3¼mm (No 10/US 3) needles and
MC, cast on 63(67) sts.
1st row (right side) P1, [K1, P1] to end.
2nd row K1, [P1, K1] to end.
Rib a further 5 rows.
Next row Rib 5 and slip these sts onto
safety pin, rib 5(4), inc in next st, [rib 6(7),
inc in next st] to last 10(9) sts, rib 5(4),
slip last 5 sts onto safety pin. 60(64) sts.
Change to 4mm (No 8/US 5) needles.
Beg with a K row, cont in st st until work
measures 14(16)cm/5½(6)in from beg,
ending with a P row.
Shape top
Next row K39(41), K2 tog tbl, turn.
Next row Sl 1 purlwise, P18, P2 tog, turn.
Next row Sl 1 purlwise, K18, K2 tog tbl,
turn.
Rep last 2 rows until all sts are decreased
on each side of centre sts, ending with a
P row. Leave rem 20 sts on a holder.

Edging
With 3¼mm (No 10/US 3) needles, right
side facing and MC, rib across 5 sts from
safety pin, pick up and K29(32) sts up
right side of hood, K across centre 20 sts,
dec one st, pick up and K29(32) sts down
left side of hood, then rib 5 sts from safety
pin. 87(93) sts.

Work 7 rows in rib. Cast off in rib.

Buttonhole Band
With 3¼mm (No 10/US 3) needles, right
side facing and MC, pick up and K12 sts
evenly along right side of hood rib and rib
edging. Work 3 rows in K1, P1 rib.
1st buttonhole row Rib 5, cast off in rib 2
sts, rib to end.
2nd buttonhole row Rib 5, cast on 2, rib
to end.
Rib 4 rows. Cast off in rib.

Button Band
Work to match Buttonhole Band omitting
buttonhole.

Ears (make 4)
With 4mm (No 8/US 5) needles and MC,
cast on 16 sts. Work 8 rows in st st. Cont
in st st, dec one st at each end of next
and 2 foll alt rows. 10 sts.
P 1 row. Cast off.

Ear Linings (make 2)
With 4mm (No 8/US 5) needles and A,
cast on 12 sts. Work in garter st (every
row K) for 6 rows. Cont in garter st, dec
one st at each end of next and foll alt row.
8 sts. Cast off.

To Make Up
With right sides of paired ear pieces
together, join seam all round, leaving cast

continued overleaf

on edges open. Turn to right side. Insert wadding and close opening. Sew ear linings in place. Sew ears to hood as shown on photograph. Sew on button.

Mittens

With 4mm (No 8/US 5) needles and MC, cast on 34 sts. K 10 rows for cuff. Work 6 rows in K1, P1 rib. Beg with a K row, cont in st st until work measures 10cm/4in from beg, ending with a P row.
Next row K1, [K2 tog tbl, K12, K2 tog] twice, K1.
P 1 row.
Next row K1, [K2 tog tbl, K10, K2 tog] twice, K1.
P 1 row. Cast off. Join seam, reversing seam on cuff. Turn back cuff.
With 4mm (No 8/US 5) needles and A,

cast on 10 sts for palm pad. Cont in garter st (every row K), work 2 rows. Inc one st at each end of next row. K 15 rows. Dec one st at each end of next row. K 2 rows. Cast off.
Sew pad in place.
Make one more.

Bootees

Upper Part
With 4mm (No 8/US 5) needles and MC, cast on 57 sts.
Beg with a K row, work 6 rows in st st.
Dec row K20, K2 tog, K13, K2 tog tbl, K20.
P 1 row.
Dec row K19, K2 tog, K13, K2 tog tbl, K19.
P 1 row.

Dec row K18, K2 tog, K13, K2 tog tbl, K18.
Cont in this way, dec 2 sts as set on every alt row until 39 sts rem.
P 1 row.
Next row K1, [P1, K1] to end.
Next row P1, [K1, P1] to end.
K 10 rows for cuff. Cast off knitwise.

Sole
With 4mm (No 8/US 5) needles and A, cast on 13 sts. K 40 rows. Cast off knitwise.

To Make Up
Join back seam of bootee, reversing seam on cuff. Sew in sole. With MC, make a cord approximately 36cm/14¼in long and thread through sts just below rib. Turn back cuff.
Make one more.

Duck Hood and Bootees

See Page
9

MATERIALS
Hood 1×50g ball of Hayfield Grampian DK in main colour (MC). Small amount of same in contrast colour (A).
Oddment of Black for embroidery.
1 button.
Bootees 1×50g ball of Hayfield Grampian DK in main colour (MC). Small amount of same in contrast colour (A).
Oddment of Black for embroidery. Pair of 3¼mm (No 10/US 3) and 4mm (No 8/US 5) knitting needles. Small amount of foam.

MEASUREMENTS
Hood To fit age
    3–6(6–9) months
Bootees To fit age
    3–9 months

TENSION
22 sts and 28 rows to 10cm/4in square over st st on 4mm (No 8/US 5) needles.

ABBREVIATIONS
K1B = K next st 1 row below.
Also see page 41.

Hood

Main Part, Edging, Buttonhole Band and Button Band
Work as given for Main Part, Edging, Buttonhole Band and Button Band of Teddy Bear Hood (see page 43).

Beak (make 2)
With 3¼mm (No 10/US 3) needles and A, cast on 19 sts. Cont in garter st (every row K), work 2 rows. Inc one st at each end of next 3 rows. Cont straight until work measures 6cm/2¼in from beg. Cast off knitwise.

To Make Up
With right sides of paired beak pieces together, join seam all round, beginning and ending 3cm/1¼in from cast off edges. Turn to right side. Cut foam to fit beak and place inside. Place top open end of beak over edging of hood at centre and bottom end and foam under the edging and slip stitch in place. Embroider eyes with Black. Sew on button.

Bootees

With 4mm (No 8/US 5) needles and MC, cast on 25 sts.
Shape sole
1st and 3 foll alt rows K.
2nd (inc) row K1, [m1, K11, m1, K1] twice.
4th (inc) row K1, m1, K12, m1, K3, m1, K12, m1, K1.
6th (inc) row K1, m1, K13, m1, K5, m1, K13, m1, K1.
8th (inc) row K1, m1, K14, m1, K7, m1, K14, m1, K1. 41 sts.
K 2 rows. Beg with a K row, work 6 rows in st st.
Next (tuck) row [K next st tog with corresponding st 6 rows below] to end.
P 1 row.

Next row (right side) K.
Next row K1, P1, [K1B, P1] to last st, K1.
Rep last 2 rows 3 times more. Beg with a K row, work 6 rows in st st.
Next (tuck) row [K next st tog with corresponding st 6 rows below] to end.
K 1 row.
Shape instep
Next row K25, turn.
Next row K9, turn.
Next row K8, K2 tog, turn.
Next row K8, K2 tog tbl, turn.
Rep last 2 rows 5 times more.
Next row K9, then K across rem 10 sts. K 1 row across all sts. 29 sts. K 6 rows.
Next row K1, [P1, K1] to end.
Next row P1, [K1, P1] to end.
Rep last 2 rows twice more, inc 4 sts evenly across last row. 33 sts.
K 8 rows for cuff. Cast off knitwise.
Join sole and side seam, reversing seam on cuff.
With 3¼mm (No 10/US 3) needles and A, cast on 14 sts for beak. K 10 rows. Cont in garter st (every row K), dec one st at each end of next and 2 foll alt rows. K 1 row. Cast off knitwise. Make one more.
With right sides of paired beak pieces together, join seam all round, beginning and ending 1cm/¼in from cast on edges. Turn to right side. Cut foam to fit beak and place inside. Place top open end of beak over top tuck of bootee and bottom end and foam under the tuck and slip stitch in place. Embroider eyes with Black. With A, make cord approximately 30cm/12in long and thread through sts of 1st row of rib. Turn back cuff. Make one more.

Mouse Hat and Bootees

MATERIALS

Hat   1×50g ball of Hayfield Grampian DK in main colour (MC). Small amount of same in each of 2 contrast colours (A and B). Pair of 4mm (No 8/US 5) knitting needles. Small amount of wadding. 1 button.

Bootees   1×50g ball of Hayfield Grampian 4 ply in main colour (MC). Small amount of same in each of 2 contrast colours (A and B). Pair each of 2¾mm (No 12/US 1) and 3¼mm (No 10/US 3) knitting needles. Small amount of wadding.

MEASUREMENTS

To fit age
    6–12 months

TENSION

22 sts and 28 rows to 10cm/4in square over st st on 4mm (No 8/US 5) needles using DK yarn.
28 sts and 36 rows to 10cm/4in square over st st on 3¼mm (No 10/US 3) needles using 4 ply yarn.

ABBREVIATIONS

See page 41.

Hat

Main Part

With 4mm (No 8/US 5) needles and MC, cast on 105 sts. K 4 rows.
1st row (right side) K1, m1, K17, sl 1, K1, psso, K1, K2 tog, K17, m1, K1, m1, K9, sl 1, K1, psso, K1, K2 tog, K9, m1, K1, m1, K17, sl 1, K1, psso, K1, K2 tog, K17, m1, K1.
2nd row P.
Rep last 2 rows 11 times more.
Shape top
1st dec row K1, K2 tog, K15, sl 1, K1, psso, K1, K2 tog, [K27, sl 1, K1, psso, K1, K2 tog] twice, K15, sl 1, K1, psso, K1.
P 1 row.
2nd dec row K16, sl 1, K1, psso, K1, K2 tog, [K25, sl 1, K1, psso, K1, K2 tog] twice, K16.
P 1 row.
3rd dec row K1, K2 tog, K12, sl 1, K1, psso, K1, K2 tog, [K23, sl 1, K1, psso, K1, K2 tog] twice, K12, sl 1, K1, psso, K1.
4th dec row P13, P2 tog, P1, P2 tog tbl, [P21, P2 tog, P1, P2 tog tbl] twice, P13.
5th dec row K12, sl 1, K1, psso, K1, K2 tog, [K19, sl 1, K1, psso, K1, K2 tog] twice, K12.

6th dec row P11, P2 tog, P1, P2 tog tbl, [P17, P2 tog, P1, P2 tog tbl] twice, P11.
7th dec row K1, K2 tog, K7, sl 1, K1, psso, K1, K2 tog, [K15, sl 1, K1, psso, K1, K2 tog] twice, K7, sl 1, K1, psso, K1.
8th dec row P8, P2 tog, P1, P2 tog tbl, [P13, P2 tog, P1, P2 tog tbl] twice, P8.
9th dec row K1, K2 tog, K4, sl 1, K1, psso, K1, K2 tog, [K11, sl 1, K1, psso, K1, K2 tog] twice, K4, sl 1, K1, psso, K1.
10th dec row P5, P2 tog, P1, P2 tog tbl, [P9, P2 tog, P1, P2 tog tbl] twice, P5.
11th dec row K4, sl 1, K1, psso, K1, K2 tog, [K7, sl 1, K1, psso, K1, K2 tog] twice, K4.
12th dec row P3, P2 tog, P1, P2 tog tbl, [P5, P2 tog, P1, P2 tog tbl] twice, P3.
13th dec row K2, sl 1, K1, psso, K1, K2 tog, [K3, sl 1, K1, psso, K1, K2 tog] twice, K2.
14th dec row P1, [P2 tog, P1, P2 tog tbl, P1] 3 times. 13 sts.
Break off yarn, thread end through rem sts, pull up and secure.

Strap

With 4mm (No 8/US 5) needles and MC, cast on 5 sts. Work in garter st (every row K) for 11cm/4½in.
Buttonhole row K1, K2 tog, yf, K2.
K 4 rows. Cast off.

Ears (make 4)

With 4mm (No 8/US 5) needles and MC, cast on 16 sts. Work 8 rows in st st. Cont in st st, dec one st at each end of next and 2 foll alt rows. 10 sts. P 1 row. Cast off.

Ear Linings (make 2)

With 4mm (No 8/US 5) needles and A, cast on 12 sts. Work in garter st for 6 rows. Cont in garter st, dec one st at each end of next and foll alt row. 8 sts. Cast off.

To Make Up

Join seam of main part. Attach cast on edge of strap to wrong side of one ear point and sew button to other in main part. With right sides of paired ear pieces together, join seam all round, leaving cast on edges open.
Turn to right side, stuff lightly and close opening. Sew ear linings in place. Sew ears to main part as shown on photograph.
With 4mm (No 8/US 5) needles and B, cast on 3 sts for nose.
Next row [K1, P1] in first st, [K1, P1, K1] in next st, [K1, P1] in last st.
K 5 rows.
Next row K2 tog, K3 tog, K2 tog.
Next row K3 tog and fasten off.

Work a running st around edge, draw up to form bobble and secure. Attach to front point on main part. With B and back st, embroider whiskers.

Bootees

With 2¾mm (No 12/US 1) needles and MC, cast on 53 sts. K 11 rows.
1st row (right side) K1, [P1, K1] to end.
2nd row P1, [K1, P1] to end.
Rep last 2 rows 3 times more.
Eyelet hole row Rib 3, [P2 tog, yrn, rib 3, K2 tog, yf, rib 3] to end.
Rib 5 rows.
Shape instep
Next row K33, turn.
Next row K13, turn.
K 22 rows on these 13 sts only. Break off yarn. Leave these sts on a holder.
With right side facing, rejoin yarn to base of instep, pick up and K12 sts evenly along side edge of instep, K13 sts from holder, then pick up and K12 sts evenly along other side edge of instep, K rem sts. 77 sts. K 17 rows. Beg with a K row, work 9 rows in st st.
Next row [P next st tog with corresponding st 9 rows below] to end.
K 13 rows for sole. Cast off.
Ears (make 4) With 3¼mm (No 10/US 3) needles and MC, cast on 16 sts. Work 8 rows in st st. Cont in st st, dec one st at each end of next and 2 foll alt rows. 10 sts. Work 1 row. Cast off.
Ear linings (make 2) With 3¼mm (No 10/US 3) needles and A, cast on 12 sts. Work in garter st (every row K) for 6 rows. Cont in garter st, dec one st at each end of next and foll alt row. 8 sts. Cast off.
Nose With 3¼mm (No 10/US 3) needles and B, cast on 3 sts.
Next row [K1, P1] in first st, [K1, P1, K1] in next st, [K1, P1] in last st.
Beg with a P row, work 5 rows in st st.
Next row K2 tog, K3 tog, K2 tog.
Next row P3 tog and fasten off.
Join seam of bootee, reversing seam on cuff. Join sole seam, folding knitting to form mitred corners. With right sides of paired ear pieces together, join seam all round, leaving cast on edges open. Turn to right side, stuff lightly and close opening. Sew ear linings in place. Attach to bootee. Work a running stitch all round nose, draw up to form bobble and secure. Attach to bootee. With B and back stitch, embroider whiskers. Make a cord approximately 40cm/15¾in long and thread through eyelet holes. Turn back cuff. Make one more.

Multi-coloured Hat and Socks

See Page
11

MATERIALS
Small amount of Hayfield Silky Cotton DK in each of Green (A), Lilac (B), Orange (C), Rust (D), Turquoise (E), Pink (F), Red (G), Purple (H) and Blue (J).
Pair each of 3¼mm (No 10/US 3) and 3¾mm (No 9/US 4) knitting needles.

MEASUREMENTS
To fit age
  3–6 (6–9) months

TENSION
24 sts and 30 rows to 10cm/4in square over st st on 3¾mm (No 9/US 4) needles.

ABBREVIATIONS
See page 41.

NOTE
Read Chart from right to left on K rows and from left to right on P rows. When working in pattern, strand yarn not in use loosely across wrong side to keep fabric elastic.

Hat

With 3¼mm (No 10/US 3) needles and A, cast on 105(117) sts.
1st row (right side) K1, [P1, K1] to end.
2nd row P1, [K1, P1] to end.
Rep last 2 rows twice more.
Change to 3¾mm (No 9/US 4) needles.
Beg with a K row and working in st st throughout, work in patt as follows:
2nd size only
Work 2 rows in J and 2 rows in H.
Both sizes
Work 2 rows in B.
Next row 1B, [2C, 2B] to end.
Next row [2B, 2C] to last st, 1B.
Next row 1D, [2E, 2D] to end.
Next row [2D, 2E] to last st, 1D.
Work 2 rows in F and 1 row in G.
Next row 2(3)G, [1E, 4G] to last 3(4) sts, 1E, 2(3)G.
Next row 2(3)G, [2E, 3G] to last 3(4) sts, 2E, 1(2)G.
Next row 0(1)G, [3E, 2G] to last 0(1) st, 0(1)E.
Next row 1(2)E, [1G, 4E] to last 4(5) sts, 1G, 3(4)E.
Work 1 row in E, 2 rows in H, 2 rows in A

and 1 row in J.
Next row 4J, [1F, 5J] to last 5 sts, 1F, 4J.
Next row 3J, [3F, 3J] to end.
Next row 1F, [1J, 5F] to last 2 sts, 1J, 1F.
Work 1 row in F, 2 rows in G, 1 row in E, dec one st at centre of last row on **1st** size only. 104(117) sts.
Shape top
Dec row With E, [K2 tog, K6(7)] to end.
Work 1 row in B.
Dec row With B, [K2 tog, K5(6)] to end.
Work 1 row in D.
Dec row With D, [K2 tog, K4(5)] to end.
Work 1 row in C.
Dec row With C, [K2 tog, K3(4)] to end.
Work 1 row in H.
Dec row With H, [K2 tog, K2(3)] to end.
Work 1 row in A.
Dec row With A, [K2, K1(2)] to end.
2nd size only
Work 1 row in B.
Dec row With B, [K2 tog, K(1)] to end.
Both sizes
Dec row With A(B), [P2 tog] to end.
13 sts.
Break off yarn, thread end through rem sts, pull up and secure. Join seam.

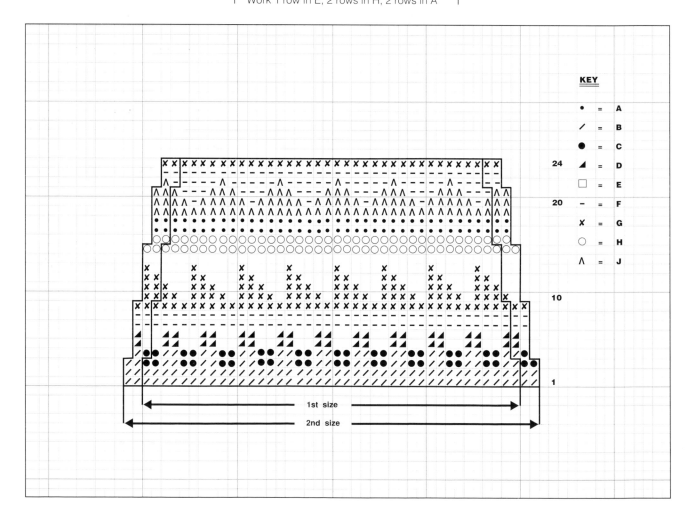

KEY

•	=	A
/	=	B
●	=	C
◢	=	D
□	=	E
–	=	F
✕	=	G
○	=	H
Λ	=	J

1st size

2nd size

Socks

With 3¼mm (No 10/US 3) needles and A, cast on 40(44) sts.
Work 6 rows in K1, P1 rib.
Change to 3¾mm (No 9/US 4) needles.
Beg with a K row and working in st st throughout, work in patt as follows:

2nd size only
Work 2 rows in J and 2 rows in H.

Both sizes
Work 1st to 24th rows of Chart, dec one st at each end of 3rd and 3 foll 6th rows. 32(36)sts.

Dec row With G, K3, [K2 tog, K6 (7)] 3 times, K2 tog, K3(4). 28(32) sts.

Shape heel
Next row With A, P8(9), turn.
Work 9 rows in st st on these 8(9) sts only.
Dec row P2(3), P2 tog, P1, turn.
Next row Sl 1, K3(4).
Dec row P3(4), P2 tog, P1, turn.
Next row Sl 1, K4(5).
Dec row P4(5), P2 tog.
Leave rem 5(6) sts on a holder.

With wrong side facing, slip centre 12(14) sts onto a holder, rejoin A yarn to rem 8(9) sts, P to end. Work 8 rows in st st on these 8(9) sts only.
Dec row K2(3), K2 tog tbl, K1, turn.
Next row Sl 1, P3(4).
Dec row K3(4), K2 tog tbl, K1, turn.
Next row Sl 1, P4(5).
Dec row K4(5), K2 tog tbl, turn.
Next row Sl 1, P4(5).

Shape instep
Change to E.
Next row K5(6), pick up and K8 sts evenly along inside edge of heel, K12(14) sts from holder, pick up and K8 sts evenly along inside edge of heel and K5(6) sts from holder. 38(42) sts. P 1 row.
Dec row K11(12), K2 tog, K12(14), K2 tog tbl, K11(12).
P 1 row.
Dec row K10(11), K2 tog, K12(14), K2 tog tbl, K10(11).
P 1 row.
Dec row K9(10), K2 tog, K12(14), K2 tog tbl, K9(10).
P 1 row.

Dec row K8(9), K2 tog, K12(14), K2 tog tbl, K8(9). 30(34) sts.
Work 11(15) rows straight. Change to A and work 2 rows.

Shape toes
Dec row K1, [K2 tog tbl, K5(6)] 4 times, K1.
P 1 row.
Dec row K1, [K2 tog tbl, K4(5)] 4 times, K1.
P 1 row.
Dec row K1, [K2 tog tbl, K3(4)] 4 times, K1.
P 1 row.
Dec row K1, [K2 tog tbl, K2(3)] 4 times, K1.

2nd size only
P 1 row.
Dec row K1, [K2 tog tbl, K(2)] 4 times, K1.

Both sizes
Dec row [P2 tog] to end. 7 sts.
Break off yarn, thread end through rem sts, pull up and secure. Join seam.
Make one more.

Crown Hat

See Page 12

MATERIALS
1 × 50g ball of Hayfield Silky Cotton DK in each of 2 colours (A and B).
Pair each of 3¾mm (No 9/US 4) and 4mm (No 8/US 5) knitting needles.

MEASUREMENTS
To fit age
6–9 (12–24) months

TENSION
22 sts and 28 rows to 10cm/4in square over st st on 4mm (No 8/US 5) needles.

ABBREVIATIONS
See page 41.

Main Part
With 4mm (No 8/US 5) needles and A, cast on 80(96) sts.
Beg with a K row, work 9(10)cm/3½(4)in in st st, ending with a P row and dec 2 sts evenly across last row on 1st size only. 78(96) sts.

Shape top
Dec row [K11(14), K2 tog] to end.
P 1 row.
Dec row [K10(13), K2 tog] to end.
P 1 row.
Dec row [K9(12), K2 tog] to end.
Cont in this way, dec 6 sts as set on every alt row until 12 sts rem.
Break off yarn, thread end through rem sts, pull up and secure.

Brim
With 3¾mm (No 9/US 4) needles, wrong side facing and B, pick up and K84(102)

sts along cast on edge of main part.
K 15(21) rows.
Work points as follows:
** **Next row** (right side) K14(17), turn.
Work on this set of sts only. K 1 row.
Next row K1, K2 tog, K to last 3 sts, K2 tog, K1.
K1 row.
Rep last 2 rows 3(5) times more.
Next row K1, [K2 tog] 2(1) times, K1(2).
K 1 row.
Next row K1, K2 tog, K1.
Cast off rem 3 sts.
With right side facing, rejoin yarn to rem sts and rep from ** until all sts are worked off.

To Make Up
Join seam, reversing seam on brim. Turn back brim and catch down each point.

Nursery Hat and Shoes

See Page
13

MATERIALS

Hat 1×50g ball of Hayfield Pure Wool Classics DK in Cream (M). Small amount of same in each of Blue (A), Green (B), Pink, Yellow, Red, Grey and Black.
Shoes 1×50g ball of Hayfield Pure Wool Classics DK in Cream (M). Small amount of same in each of Blue (A), Green (B), Pink and Yellow. Pair each of 3¾mm (No 9/US 4) and 4mm (No 8/US 5) knitting needles.

MEASUREMENTS

To fit age
    6–12 months

TENSION

22 sts and 28 rows to 10cm/4in square over st st on 4mm (No 8/US 5) needles.

ABBREVIATIONS

See page 41.

NOTE

Read Charts from right to left on K rows and from left to right on P rows unless otherwise stated. When working motifs, use separate lengths of yarn for each coloured area and twist yarns together on wrong side at joins to avoid holes.

Hat

With 4mm (No 8/US 5) needles and M, cast on 91 sts.
1st row (right side) K1, [P1, K1] to end.
2nd row P1, [K1, P1] to end.
K 1 row.
Stranding yarn not in use loosely across wrong side over no more than 4 sts at a time, work brim patt as follows:
1st row (wrong side) P3M, 1A, [6M, 1B, 6M, 1A] to last 3 sts, 3M.
2nd row K2M, 3A, [4M, 3B, 4M, 3A] to last 2 sts, 2M.
3rd row P1M, 5A, [2M, 5B, 2M, 5A] to last st, 1M.
4th row K7A, [7B, 7A] to end.

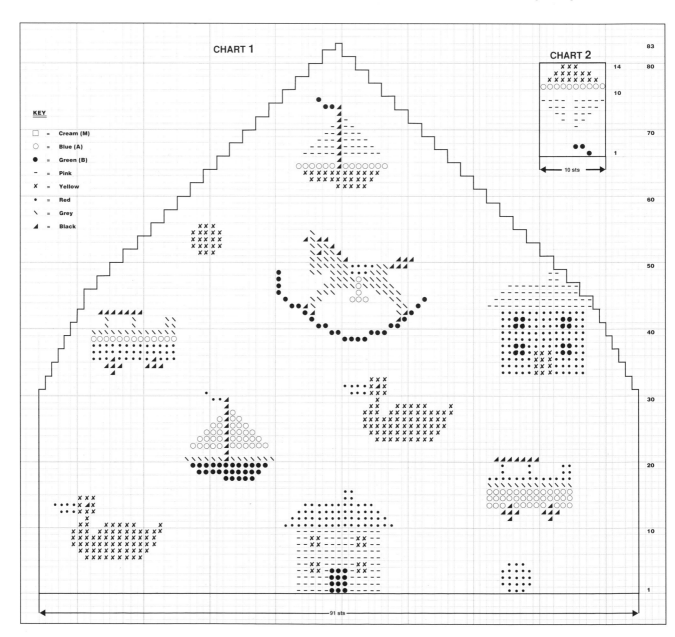

With M, work a further 2 rows in st st.
Beg with a K row (thus reversing fabric), work 8 rows in st st.
Cont in st st and patt from Chart 1 until 30th row of Chart 1 has been worked.
Shape top
Cont working from Chart 1, dec one st at each end of next and 6 foll alt rows. Work 1 row. Cast off 2 sts at beg of every row until 1 st rem. Fasten off. Join seam, reversing seam on brim. Turn back brim.

Shoes

With 3¾mm (No 9/US 4) needles and M, cast on 42 sts.
K 4 rows. Beg with a K row, work 2 rows in st st.
Stranding yarn not in use loosely across wrong side over no more than 4 sts at a time, work cuff patt as follows:
1st row (right side) [K7A, 7B] to end.
2nd row [P1M, 5B, 2M, 5A, 1M] to end.
3rd row [K2M, 3A, 4M, 3B, 2M] to end.
4th row [P3M, 1B, 6M, 1A, 3M] to end.
Cont in M, K 3 rows, then work 10 rows in K1, P1 rib, inc one st at centre of last row. 43 sts.

Beg with a K row (thus reversing fabric), work 4 rows in st st.
Shape instep
Next row K28, turn.
Next row P13, turn.
Work on these 13 sts only. Cont in st st, work 1st to 14th rows of Chart 2. With M, work 2 rows in st st. Break off yarn and leave these sts on a holder.
With right side facing, rejoin M at base of instep, pick up and K10 sts evenly along side edge of instep, K across 13 sts on holder, pick up and K10 sts evenly along other side edge of instep, K rem 15 sts. 63 sts.
K 8 rows.
Next row [K next st tog with corresponding st 7 rows below] to end.
Beg with a K row, work 2 rows in st st.
Now work patt as follows:
1st row K3M, [1A, 6M, 1B, 6M] to last 4 sts, 1A, 3M.
2nd row P2M, 3A, [4M, 3B, 4M, 3A] to last 2 sts, 2M.
3rd row K1M, [5A, 2M, 5B, 2M] to last 6 sts, 5A, 1M.
4th row P7A, [7B, 7A] to end.
With M, work 2 rows in st st. Break off yarn.
Shape sole
With right side facing, slip first 25 sts

onto right hand needle, rejoin M and work as follows:
Next row K12, K2 tog, turn.
Next row Sl 1, K11, K2 tog tbl, turn.
Next row Sl 1, K11, K2 tog, turn.
Rep last 2 rows 10 times more, then work first of the 2 rows again.
Next row Sl 1, K4, sl 1, K2 tog, psso, K4, K2 tog, turn.
Next row Sl 1, K9, K2 tog tbl, turn.
Next row Sl 1, K9, K2 tog, turn.
Rep last 2 rows once more, then work first of the 2 rows again.
Next row Sl 1, K3, sl 1, K2 tog, psso, K3, K2 tog, turn.
Next row Sl 1, K7, K2 tog tbl, turn.
Next row Sl 1, K7, K2 tog, turn.
Rep last 2 rows 4 times more.
Next row Sl 1, K3, K2 tog, K2, K2 tog tbl.
Place rem 4 sts at each side of sole on one needle, pointing in the same direction as needle with sole sts. With right sides of sole and upper sts together, cast off together rem 8 sts.
Join seam, reversing seam on cuff. Turn back cuff.
Make one more, reversing cuff patt by using A instead of B and B instead of A and Chart 2 position by reading K rows from left to right and P rows from right to left.

Christmas Pudding Hat and Mittens

See Page 14

MATERIALS
1 × 50g ball of Hayfield Grampian DK in each of Brown (A) and Cream (B). Small amount of same in each of Green (C) and Red (D).
Pair each of 4mm (No 8/US 5) and 6mm (No 4/US 9) knitting needles.

MEASUREMENTS
To fit age
6–12 months

TENSION
16 sts and 22 rows to 10cm/4in square over st st on 6mm (No 4/US 9) needles using two strands of yarn together.
22 sts and 28 rows to 10cm/4in square over st st on 4mm (No 8/US 5) needles.

ABBREVIATIONS
See page 41.

Hat

With 6mm (No 4/US 9) needles and two strands of A together, cast on 74 sts.
Beg with a K row, work 22 rows in st st.
Stranding yarn not in use loosely across wrong side over no more than 3 sts at a time and using two strands of B together, work in patt as follows:
1st row (right side) K11A, [5B, 19A] twice, 5B, 10A.
2nd row P8A, [9B, 15A] twice, 9B, 9A.
3rd row K8A, [11B, 13A] twice, 11B, 7A.
4th row P5A, [15B, 9A] twice, 15B, 6A.
5th row K4A, [19B, 5A] twice, 19B, 3A.
Cont in st st and B only, work 1 row.
Shape top
Dec row K2, [K2 tog, K10] to end.

P 1 row.
Dec row K2, [K2 tog, K9] to end.
P 1 row.
Dec row K2, [K2 tog, K8] to end.
Cont in this way, dec 6 sts as set on every alt row until 44 sts rem.
P 1 row.
Dec row [K2 tog] to end.
Break off yarn, thread end through rem sts, pull up and secure. Join seam, reversing seam on last 5cm/2in for brim. Roll back brim.
Holly leaves (make 6) With 4mm (No 8/US 5) needles and C, cast on 13 sts.
Beg with a K row, work 4 rows in st st.
Picot row K1, [yf, K2 tog] to end.
Beg with a P row, work 4 rows in st st.
Cast off row P first st tog with corresponding st of cast on row, [P next

st on left hand needle with corresponding st of cast on row, then pass 2nd st on right hand needle over first st] to end.
Fasten off. Join ends and cast off edges of leaves in pairs. Attach to top of hat.
Berries (make 3) With 4mm (No 8/US 5) needles and D, cast on 1 st.
Next row [K1, P1, K1, P1, K1] all in st.
P 1 row, K 1 row.
Next row P2 tog, P1, P2 tog.
Next row Sl 1, K2 tog, psso.
Fasten off. Work a running st around edge, draw up to form bobble and secure. Form berries into a bunch and attach to top of hat.

Mittens

With 4mm (No 8/US 5) needles and B, cast on 36 sts.
K 8 rows for cuff. Work 4 rows in K1, P1 rib.
Beg with a K row, work 8 rows in st st.
Stranding yarn not in use loosely across wrong side over no more than 4 sts at a time, work in patt as follows:
1st row (right side) K3A, 12B, 6A, 12B, 3A.
2nd row P5A, 8B, 10A, 8B, 5A.
3rd row K7A, 4B, 14A, 4B, 7A.
Cont in st st and A only, work 7 rows.

continued overleaf

Dec row K2, [K2 tog tbl, K11, K2 tog, K2]
twice.
P 1 row.
Dec row K2, [K2 tog tbl, K9, K2 tog, K2]
twice.
P 1 row.
Dec row K2, [K2 tog tbl, K7, K2 tog, K2]
twice.
P 1 row. Cast off. Join side seam,
reversing seam on cuff. Turn back cuff.
With B, make a cord approximately

32cm/12½in long. Thread through sts just
below rib, beginning and ending at centre
of top part of mitten. Make 2 berries as
given for Hat and attach one to each end
of cord. Tie into a bow.
Leaves (make 4) With 4mm (No 8/US 5)
needles and C, cast on 11 sts.
Beg with a K row, work 2 rows in st st.
Picot row K1, [yf, K2 tog] to end.
Beg with a P row, work 2 rows in st st.
Cast off row P first st tog with

corresponding st of cast on row, [P next
st on left hand needle tog with
corresponding st of cast on row, then
pass 2nd st on right hand needle over
first st] to end.
Fasten off. Join ends and cast off edges
of leaves in pairs. Attach to cuff above
tied cord.
Make one more.

Mexican Poncho with Pompons and Hat

See Page
15

MATERIALS
Poncho 2×50g balls of Hayfield
Pure Wool Classics DK in Red (M).
Small amount of same in each of
Blue, Gold, Black, Pink, Green and
Yellow.
Pair of 4mm (No 8/US 5) knitting
needles.
Hat 1×50g ball of Hayfield Grampian
DK.
Pair of 6mm (No 4/US 9) knitting
needles.

MEASUREMENTS
To fit age
    1 year
Width of poncho
    30cm/12in
Length of poncho
    30cm/12in.

TENSION
22 sts and 28 rows to 10cm/4in
square over st st on 4mm (No 8/US
5) needles.
16 sts and 22 rows to 10cm/4in
square over st st on 6mm (No 4/US
9) needles using two strands of yarn
together.

ABBREVIATIONS
See page 41.

NOTE
Read Chart from right to left on K
rows and from left to right on P rows.
When working motifs, use separate
lengths of yarn for each coloured
area and twist yarns together on
wrong side at joins to avoid holes.

Poncho

Beg at lower edge of Front.
With 4mm (No 8/US 5) needles and M,
cast on 68 sts. K 4 rows.
Next row K.
Next row K2, P64, K2.
Rep last 2 rows twice more.
Work patt from Chart as follows:

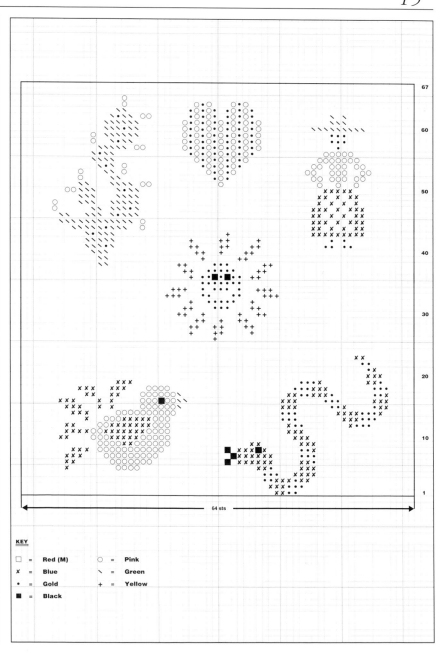

KEY
☐ = Red (M)   ○ = Pink
✕ = Blue   \ = Green
• = Gold   + = Yellow
■ = Black

64 sts

Next row K2M, K across 1st row of Chart, K2M.
Next row K2M, P across 2nd row of Chart, K2M.
Cont working from Chart as set until 67th row of Chart has been worked.
Cont in M only.
Shape neck
Next row K2, P15, K34, P15, K2.
K 1 row.
Next row K2, P15, K34, P15, K2.
Next row K20, cast off 28, K to end.
Work on last set of sts only.
Next row K2, P15, K3.
Next row K.
Rep last 2 rows twice more, then work 1st of the 2 rows again. Leave these sts on a spare needle.
With wrong side facing, rejoin yarn to rem sts.
Next row K3, P15, K2.
Next row K.
Rep last 2 rows twice more, then work 1st of the 2 rows again.

Next row K to end, cast on 28 sts, K across sts on spare needle.
Next row K2, P15, K34, P15, K2.
K1 row. Rep last 2 rows once.
Next row K2, P68, K2.
Now turn Chart upside down and work from it as follows:
Next row K2M, K across 65th row of Chart, K2M.
Next row K2M, P across 64th row of Chart, K2M.
Cont working from Chart as set until 1st row of Chart has been worked.
Cont in M only.
Next row K2, P68, K2.
Next row K.
Rep last 2 rows twice more. K 4 rows.
Cast off knitwise.
With Black, work a border of blanket st inside garter st edging of poncho.
Make pompons in each of Blue, Pink, Green and Yellow and attach one securely to each corner.

Hat

With 6mm (No 4/US 9) needles and two strands of yarn together, cast on 74 sts.
Beg with a K row, work 28 rows in st st.
Shape top
Dec row K2, [K2 tog, K10] to end.
P 1 row.
Dec row K2, [K2 tog, K9] to end.
P 1 row.
Dec row K2, [K2 tog, K8] to end.
Cont in this way, dec 6 sts as set on every foll alt row until 44 sts rem.
P 1 row.
Dec row [K2 tog] to end.
Break off yarn, thread end through rem sts, pull up and secure. Join seam, reversing seam on last 5cm/2in for brim.
Roll back brim.

Inca Hat and Socks

See Page 16

MATERIALS
1 × 50g ball of Hayfield Pure Wool Classics DK or Hayfield Grampian DK in Pink (A).
Small amount of same in each of Green (B), Yellow (C), Blue (D), Navy (E), Cream (F), Red (G) and White (H).
Pair of 4mm (No 8/US 5) knitting needles.
One 3¾mm (No 9/US 4) circular needle for hat.
Pair of 3¼mm (No 10/US 3) knitting needles for socks.

MEASUREMENTS
Hat To fit age
6–12 (18–24) months
Socks To fit age
6–12 months

TENSION
22 sts and 28 rows to 10cm/4in square over st st on 4mm (No 8/US 5) needles.

ABBREVIATIONS
See page 41.

NOTE
Read Chart from right to left on K rows and from left to right on P rows. When working in pattern, strand yarn not in use loosely across wrong side over no more than 4 sts at a time to keep fabric elastic.

Hat

Ear Flaps (make 2)
With 4mm (No 8/US 5) needles and E, cast on 6(8) sts.
Beg with a K row and working in st st throughout, work 2 rows E, 2 rows D, 2 rows B, **at the same time**, inc one st at each end of every row. 18(20) sts.
Work 2 rows C, 2 rows H, 2 rows G and 2 rows A.
Now work 2 rows E, 2 rows D and 2 rows B, **at the same time**, dec one st at each end of first and 2 foll alt rows. 12(14) sts.
Work 2 rows C.
Work 2 rows H and 2 rows G, inc one st at each end of first and foll alt row. 16(18) sts. Leave these sts on a holder.

Main Part
With 4mm (No 8/US 5) needles and A, cast on 10(12) sts, K across 16(18) sts of one ear flap, cast on 39(43) sts, K across 16(18) sts of other ear flap, cast on 10(12) sts. 91(103) sts.
Cont in st st, work 1 row A, 2 rows E, 2 rows D, 2 rows B, 2 rows C, 2 rows H and 2 rows G.
Inc row With A, K1(3), [m1, K15(10)] to end. 97(113) sts.
Work 1 row A.
Now work 1st to 15th rows of Chart. Work 2 rows A.
Shape top
Dec row With G, P2(3), [P2 tog, P3] to end.
Work 1 row G and 2 rows H.

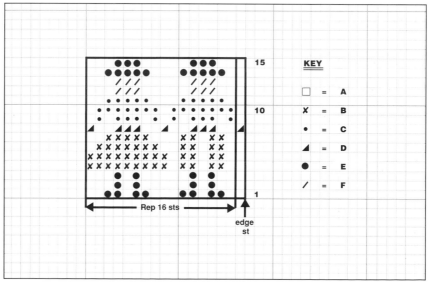

KEY		
□	=	A
X	=	B
•	=	C
◢	=	D
●	=	E
/	=	F

Rep 16 sts

edge st

continued overleaf

Dec row With C, P2(3), [P2 tog, P2] to end.
Work 1 row C and 2(4) rows B.
Dec row With B, P2(0), [P2 tog, P1] to end.
Work 3 rows B. Cont in D only.
Dec row [P2 tog] to end.
Work 1 row.
Dec row P0(1), [P2 tog] to end. 10(12) sts.
Work 4 rows. Break off yarn, thread end through rem sts, pull up and secure.

Lower Edging

With 3¼mm (No 9/US 4) circular needle, right side facing and H, pick up and K1 st for each cast on st along cast on edges and 44(46) sts around each ear flap. 147(159) sts. Work backwards and forwards, K 2 rows. Cast off knitwise. Join seam.

Socks

With 3¼mm (No 10/US 3) needles and D, cast on 35 sts.
1st row (right side) K1, [P1, K1] to end.
2nd row P1, [K1, P1] to end.
Rep last 2 rows once more.
Change to 4mm (No 8/US 5) needles.
Beg with a K row and working in st st throughout, work 2 rows B, 2 rows C, 2

rows H, 2 rows G and 2 rows A, inc 6 sts evenly across last row. 41 sts.
Work patt from Chart as follows:
1st row Work edge st of 15th row of Chart, rep the 16 sts twice, work first 7 sts of the 16 sts, then work edge st again.
2nd row Work edge st of 14th row of Chart, work last 7 sts of the 16 sts, rep the 16 sts twice, then work edge st again.
Cont working from Chart as set, work 13th to 1st rows.
Work 2 rows A, dec 7 sts evenly across last row. 34 sts. Work 2 rows G.
Shape heel
Next row With D, P9, turn.
Cont in D on these 9 sts only, work 7 rows.
Dec row P3, P2 tog, turn.
Next row and foll alt row Sl 1, K to end.
Dec row P4, P2 tog, turn.
Dec row P5, P2 tog.
Leave rem 6 sts on a holder.
With wrong side facing, slip centre 16 sts onto a holder, rejoin D to rem 9 sts, P to end. Cont in D on these 9 sts only, work 6 rows.
Dec row K3, K2 tog tbl, turn.
Next row and foll alt row Sl 1, P to end.
Dec row K4, K2 tog tbl, turn.
Dec row K5, K2 tog tbl, turn.
Next row Sl 1, P to end.
Shape instep
Next row With H, K6, pick up and K8 sts

along inside edge of heel, K16 sts from holder, pick up and K8 sts along inside edge of heel, K6 sts from holder. 44 sts.
Work 1 row H.
Dec row With C, K12, K2 tog, K16, K2 tog tbl, K12.
Work 1 row C.
Dec row With B, K11, K2 tog, K16, K2 tog tbl, K11.
Work 1 row B.
Dec row With D, K10, K2 tog, K16, K2 tog tbl, K10.
Work 1 row D.
Dec row With E, K9, K2 tog, K16, K2 tog tbl, K9. 36 sts.
Work 1 row E, 2 rows A, 2 rows G, 2 rows H and 2 rows C. Cont in B only work 2 rows.
Shape toes
Dec row [Sl 1, K1, psso, K7] 4 times.
Work 1 row.
Dec row [Sl 1, K1, psso, K6] 4 times.
Work 1 row.
Dec row [Sl 1, K1, psso, K5] 4 times.
Cont in this way, dec 4 sts as set on every alt row until 12 sts rem.
Work 1 row.
Dec row [K2 tog] to end.
Break off yarn, thread end through rem sts, pull up and secure. Join seam.
Make one more.

Ladybird Hat and Slippers

See Page
17

MATERIALS
Hat 1×50g ball of Hayfield Grampian DK in Red (MC).
Small amount of same in Black (A).
2 pipe cleaners.
Slippers 1×50g ball of Hayfield Grampian DK in Red (MC).
Small amount of same in Black (A).
2 buttons.
Pair each of 3¼mm (No 10/US 3) and 4mm (No 8/US 5) knitting needles.

MEASUREMENTS
To fit age
   6–12 months

TENSION
22 sts and 28 rows to 10cm/4in square over st st on 4mm (No 8/US 5) needles.

ABBREVIATIONS
See page 41.

Hat

Main Part

Work as given for Main Part of Mouse Hat (see page 45).

Spots (make 5)

With 4mm (No 8/US 5) needles and A, cast on 8 sts. Work in garter st (every row K) inc one st at each end of 3rd and 2 foll alt rows. K 8 rows. Dec one st at each end of next and 2 foll alt rows. K 2 rows. Cast off knitwise.

Feelers (make 2)

With 4mm (No 8/US 5) needles and A, cast on 9 sts. Work 10cm/4in in st st. Cast off.

To Make Up

Join back seam of main part. Sew on spots. Fold feelers lengthwise and join seam. Insert pipe cleaners and close up ends. Attach to front point of main part.

Slippers

With 3¼mm (No 10/US 3) needles and MC, cast on 18 sts.
Work in garter st (every row K) throughout, inc one st at each end of every alt row until there are 32 sts. Dec one st at each end of next and every alt row until 18 sts rem.
Next row Cast on 7 sts for heel, K to end. 25 sts.
Inc one st at end of 6 foll alt rows. 31 sts.
K 1 row.

Next row Cast off knitwise 17 sts (mark 9th st of these sts), K to last st, inc in last st. K 12 rows.
Next row K2 tog, K to end, turn and cast on 17 sts (mark 9th st of these sts). 31 sts.
Dec one st at beg of 6 foll alt rows. 25 sts.
K1 row. Cast off knitwise.
Join back heel seam.
With 3¼mm (No 10/US 3) needles, A and right side facing, pick up and K9 sts from marker to back seam and 9 sts from back seam to next marker. 18 sts.
Next row Cast on 14 sts, K to end, turn and cast on 14 sts.
K 2 rows.
1st buttonhole row K2, cast off 3, K to end.
2nd buttonhole row K to last 2 sts, cast on 3, K2.
K 2 rows. Cast off knitwise.
Fold slipper along row just below cast on sts for heel and, with right sides together, join seam all round, easing in fullness at toes and sewing the 7 cast on sts and last 7 sts of cast off edge to sole. Turn to right side.
With 4mm (No 8/US 5) needles and A, cast on 6 sts for spot. Work in garter st, inc one st at each end of 2 foll alt rows. K2 rows.
Dec one st at each end of next and foll alt row. K 1 row. Cast off knitwise.
Make 2 more spots. Sew on spots and button.
Make one more, reversing buttonhole rows.

Reindeer Hat, Scarf, Mittens and Socks

See Page
18

MATERIALS
4 × 50g balls of Hayfield Grampian DK in Black (M) and 2 × 50g balls in Cream (A).
Small amount of same in Red (C).
Pair of 4mm (No 8/US 5) knitting needles. Medium-size crochet hook.

MEASUREMENTS
To fit age
  6–12 months

TENSION
24 sts and 25 rows to 10cm/4in square over Fair Isle pattern on 4mm (No 8/US 5) needles.

ABBREVIATIONS
See page 41.

NOTE
Read Charts from right to left on K rows and from left to right on P rows unless otherwise stated. When working in pattern, strand yarn not in use loosely across wrong side over no more than 5 sts at a time to keep fabric elastic.

Hat

With 4mm (No 8/US 5) needles and M, cast on 97 sts
1st row K1, [P1, K1] to end.
2nd row P1, [K1, P1] to end.
Beg with a K row and 1st row of Chart 1, work 9 rows in st st and patt from Chart 1 for brim. With M, P 2 rows.
Beg with a K row and 1st row of Chart 1, work 55 rows in st st and patt from Chart 1. Cont in M only, P 1 row.
Shape top
Dec row K1, [K2 tog, K6] 12 times.
P 1 row.
Dec row K1, [K2 tog, K5] 12 times.
P 1 row.
Dec row K1, [K2 tog, K4] 12 times.
Cont in this way, dec 12 sts as set on every alt row until 25 sts rem, ending with a P row.
Dec row K1, [K2 tog] 12 times. 13 sts.
Break off yarn, thread end through rem sts, pull up and secure. Join seam, reversing seam on brim. With C, make a large pompon and attach to top. Turn back brim.

Scarf

With 4mm (No 8/US 5) needles and M, cast on 49 sts. Beg with a K row, work 8 rows in st st. Cont in st st and patt from Chart 1, work 1st to 61st rows, then 1st to

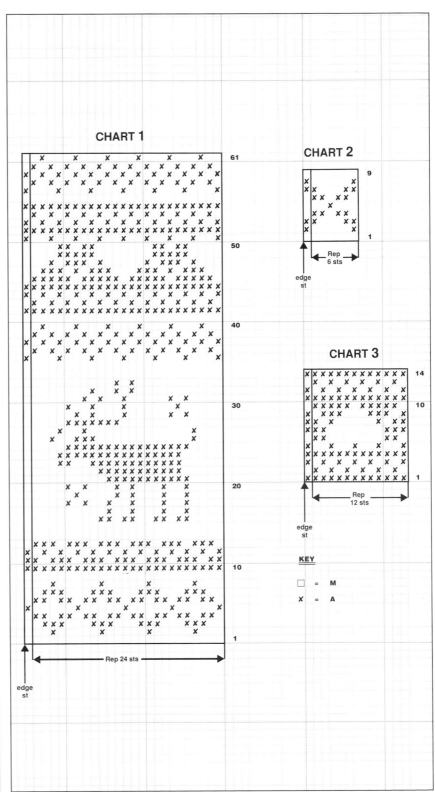

continued overleaf

35th rows. Turn Chart 1 upside down. Now reading Chart 1 from left to right on K rows and from right to left on P rows and working rows in reverse order, work 35th to 1st rows, then 61st to 1st rows. With M only, work 8 rows in st st. Cast off. Fold scarf in half lengthwise and join long seam. Gather short ends, draw up and secure. With C, make 2 pompons and attach to each end.

Mittens

With 4mm (No 8/US 5) needles and M, cast on 37 sts.
1st row K1, [P1, K1] to end.
2nd row P1, [K1, P1] to end.
Beg with a K row and 1st row of Chart 2, work 9 rows in st st and patt from Chart 2 for cuff.
Cont in M, P 1 row, then rep 1st and 2nd rows 6 times.
Beg with a P row, work 4 rows in st st.
Cont in st st and patt from Chart 3, work 1st to 14th rows. Cont in M only, P 1 row.
Dec row K2, [K2 tog tbl, K12, K2 tog, K1] twice, K1.
P 1 row.
Dec row K2, [K2 tog tbl, K10, K2 tog, K1] twice, K1.
P 1 row.
Cast off. Make one more.
Join side seams, reversing seams on cuffs.
With crochet hook and using C yarn double, make a chain cord approximately

80cm/31½in long. Make 2 pompons with C and sew to each end of cord. Attach cord to each mitten as shown on photograph. Turn back cuffs.

Socks

With 4mm (No 8/US 5) needles and M, cast on 37 sts.
1st row K1, [P1, K1] to end.
2nd row P1, [K1, P1] to end.
Beg with a K row and 1st row of Chart 2, work 9 rows in st st and patt from Chart 2 for cuff.
Cont in M only, P1 row, then rep 1st and 2nd rows 6 times. P 1 row. Beg with a K row and 1st row of Chart 3, work 14 rows in st st and patt from Chart 3. Cont in M only, K 1 row, dec 3 sts evenly across last row. 34 sts.
Shape heel
Next row P9, turn.
Work 7 rows in st st on these 9 sts only.
Dec row P3, P2 tog, turn.
Next row Sl 1, K3.
Dec row P4, P2 tog, turn.
Next row Sl 1, K4.
Dec row P5, P2 tog.
Leave rem 6 sts on a holder.
With wrong side facing, slip centre 16 sts onto a holder, rejoin yarn to rem 9 sts, P to end. Work 6 rows in st st on these 9 sts only.
Dec row K3, K2 tog tbl, turn.
Next row Sl 1, P3.
Dec row K4, K2 tog tbl, turn.

Next row Sl 1, P4.
Dec row K5, K2 tog tbl, turn.
Next row Sl 1, P5.
Shape instep
Next row K6, pick up and K8 sts along inside edge of heel, K16 sts from holder, pick up and K8 sts along inside edge of heel, K6 sts from holder. 44 sts.
P 1 row.
Dec row K12, K2 tog, K16, K2 tog tbl, K12.
P 1 row.
Dec row K11, K2 tog, K16, K2 tog tbl, K11.
P 1 row.
Dec row K10, K2 tog, K16, K2 tog tbl, K10.
Cont in this way, dec 2 sts as set on every alt row until 34 sts rem.
Work 15 rows straight.
Shape toes
Dec row K1, [sl 1, K1, psso, K6] 4 times, K1.
P 1 row.
Dec row K1, [sl 1, K1, psso, K5] 4 times, K1.
P 1 row.
Dec row K1, [sl 1, K1, psso, K4] 4 times, K1.
Cont in this way, dec 4 sts as set on every alt row until 14 sts rem.
Dec row [P2 tog] 7 times.
Break off yarn, thread end through rem sts, pull up and secure. Join seam, reversing seam on cuff. Turn back cuff. Make one more.

Scandinavian Hat, Mittens and Socks with Tassels

See
Front Cover

MATERIALS
2×50g balls of Hayfield Pure Wool Classics DK or Hayfield Grampian DK in main colour (M).
1×50g ball of same in each of 2 contrast colours (A and B).
Pair of 4mm (No 8/US 5) knitting needles.

MEASUREMENTS
Hat and mittens To fit age
  9–18 months
Socks To fit age
  9–12 months

TENSION
22 sts and 28 rows to 10cm/4in square over st st on 4mm (No 8/US 5) needles.

ABBREVIATIONS
See page 41.

NOTE
Read Chart from right to left on K rows and from left to right on P rows. When working motifs, use separate lengths of yarn for each coloured area and twist yarns together on wrong side at joins to avoid holes.

Leave these sts on a spare needle. Work one more.
With right sides together, cast off top sts together by taking one st from each needle and knitting them together. Join side seams, reversing seams on brim. Turn back brim. With A, make 2 tassels and attach one to each corner of hat.

Mittens

With 4mm (No 8/US 5) needles and M, cast on 36 sts.
Work as given for Hat from ** to **.
Now work 10 rows in K1, P1 rib.
Beg with a P row (thus reversing fabric), work 7 rows in st st.
Place heart motif as follows:
1st row K4M, K 10th to 20th sts of 36th row of Chart, K21M.
2nd row P21M, P 20th to 10th sts of 35th row of Chart, P4M.
Cont working heart motif from Chart in reverse order as set, work a further 9 rows.
With M only, work 5 rows in st st. Change

Hat

With 4mm (No 8/US 5) needles and M, cast on 48 sts.
** Work 2 rows in K1, P1 rib. K 1 row. Stranding yarn not in use loosely across wrong side, work brim patt as follows:
1st row (wrong side) [P3A, 3M] to end.
2nd row [K3M, 3A] to end.

3rd row As 1st row.
4th row [K3A, 3M] to end.
5th row [P3M, 3A] to end.
6th row As 4th row.
P 1 row. **
Beg with a P row (thus reversing fabric), work 17 rows in st st.
Cont in st st and patt from Chart until 36th row of Chart has been worked.
With M only, work a further 4 rows in st st.

to A and work 2 rows in st st.
Dec row [K1, K2 tog tbl, K12, K2 tog, K1] twice.
P 1 row.
Dec row [K1, K2 tog tbl, K10, K2 tog, K1] twice. Cast off.
Make 3 bobbles around heart motif. To make bobble, attach B yarn to right side of st where bobble is to be worked, work bobble as given on Chart, fasten off. Pull ends to wrong side and secure.
Join side seam, reversing seam on cuff. Turn back cuff. With A, make a tassel and attach securely to centre of front cuff.
Make one more, placing heart motif in reverse position as follows:
1st row K21M, K 10th to 20th sts of 36th row of Chart, K4M.
2nd row P4M, P 20th to 10th sts of 35th row of Chart, P21M.

Socks

With 4mm (No 8/US 5) needles and M, cast on 36 sts.
Work as given for Hat from ** to **.
Now work 10 rows in K1, P1 rib, dec one st at centre. 35 sts.
Beg with a P row (thus reversing fabric), work 7 rows in st st.
Place snowflake motif as follows:
1st row K11M, K 29th to 41st sts of 5th

row of Chart, K11M.
2nd row P11M, P41st to 29th sts of 6th P11M, P41st to row of Chart, P11M.
Cont working snowflake motif from Chart as set, work a further 11 rows.
Cont in M only, work 2 rows in st st, dec one st at end of last row. 34 sts.
Shape heel
Next row P9, turn.
Work 9 rows in st st on these 9 sts only.
Dec row P3, P2 tog, turn.
Next row and foll alt row Sl 1, K to end.
Dec row P4, P2 tog, turn.
Dec row P5, P2 tog.
Leave rem 6 sts on a holder.
With wrong side facing, slip centre 16 sts onto a holder, rejoin yarn to rem 9 sts, P to end. Work 8 rows on these 9 sts only.
Dec row K3, K2 tog tbl, turn.
Next row and foll alt row Sl 1, P to end.
Dec row K4, K2 tog tbl, turn.
Dec row K5, K2 tog tbl, turn.
Next row Sl 1, P5.
Shape instep
Next row K6, pick up and K8 sts along inside edge of heel, K16 sts from holder, pick up and K8 sts along inside edge of heel, K6 sts from holder.
44 sts.
P 1 row.
Dec row K12, K2 tog, K16, K2 tog tbl, K12.
P 1 row.

Dec row K11, K2 tog, K16, K2 tog tbl, K11.
P 1 row.
Dec row K10, K2 tog, K16, K2 tog tbl, K10.
Cont in this way, dec 2 sts as set on every alt row until 34 sts rem.
Work 13 rows straight.
Change to A and work 2 rows.
Shape toes
Dec row K1, [sl 1, K1, psso, K6] 4 times, K1.
P 1 row.
Dec row K1, [sl 1, K1, psso, K5] 4 times, K1.
P 1 row.
Dec row K1, [sl 1, K1, psso, K4] 4 times, K1.
Cont in this way, dec 4 sts as set on every alt row until 14 sts rem.
Dec row [P2 tog] 7 times.
Break off yarn, thread end through rem sts, pull up and secure. Make 3 bobbles around snowflake motif. To make bobble, attach B yarn to right side of st where bobble is to be worked, work bobble as given on Chart, fasten off. Pull ends to wrong side and secure. Join seam, reversing seam on cuff. Turn back cuff. With A, make a tassel and attach to centre of outside cuff.
Make one more.

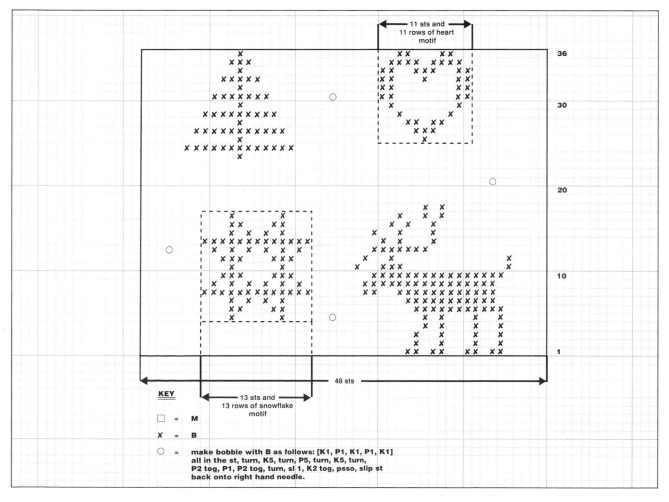

KEY

□ = M

X = B

○ = **make bobble with B as follows: [K1, P1, K1, P1, K1]
all in the st, turn, K5, turn, P5, turn, K5, turn,
P2 tog, P1, P2 tog, turn, sl 1, K2 tog, psso, slip st
back onto right hand needle.**

Christmas Tree Hat

See Page 19

MATERIALS

1(1: 2) × 50g balls of Hayfield Grampian DK in main colour (MC). Oddment of same in each of Red, Turquoise and Pink. Small amount of DK lurex yarn. Small piece of Yellow felt, 5 tiny plastic dolls, 3 rocking horse buttons, 2 teddy bear buttons, 1 car button, 5 gold balls and 8 plastic stars. Pair each of 3mm (No 11/US 2) and 3¼mm (No 10/US 3) knitting needles. Medium-size crochet hook.

MEASUREMENTS

To fit age
1(2–3: 4–6) years

TENSION

28 sts and 36 rows to 10cm/4in square over st st on 3¼mm (No 10/US 3) needles.

ABBREVIATIONS

See page 41.

To Make

With 3¼mm (No 10/US 3) needles and MC, cast on 147(163: 179) sts.
1st row (right side) K1, [P1, K1] to end.
2nd row P1, [K1, P1] to end.
Cont in rib, work 2 rows.
Dec row Rib 29(33: 37), P3 tog, K1, P3 tog tbl, rib 75(83: 91), P3 tog, K1, P3 tog tbl, rib 29(33: 37).
Rib 1 row.

Dec row Rib 27(31: 35), P3 tog, K1, P3 tog tbl, rib 71(79: 87), P3 tog, K1, P3 tog tbl, rib 27(31: 35).
Rib 1 row.
Dec row Rib 25(29: 33), P3 tog, K1, P3 tog tbl, rib 67(75: 83), P3 tog, K1, P3 tog tbl, rib 25(29: 33).
Cont in this way, dec 8 sts as set on every alt row until 107(123: 139) sts rem, ending with a wrong side row.
Next row K24(28: 32), yf, sl 1, yb, turn.
Next row Sl 1, P3, yb, sl 1, yf, turn.
Next row Sl 1, K5, yf, sl 1, yb, turn.
Next row Sl 1, P7, yb, sl 1, yf, turn.
Cont in this way, working 2(2: 3) sts more at end of every row until the row "Sl 1, P27(11: 31), yb, sl 1, yf, turn" has been worked, then working 3 sts more at end of every row until the row "Sl 1, P45(53: 61)" has been worked.
Next row K across all sts.
Next row P24(28: 32), yb, sl 1, yf, turn.
Next row Sl 1, K3, yf, sl 1, yb, turn.
Next row Sl 1, P5, yb, sl 1, yf, turn.
Next row Sl 1, K7, yf, sl 1, yb, turn.
Cont in this way, working 2(2: 3) sts more at end of every row until the row "Sl 1, K27(11: 31), yf, sl 1, yb, turn" has been worked, then working 3 sts more at end of every row until the row "Sl 1, K45(53: 61)" has been worked. Beg with a P row, work 7(11: 15) rows in st st across all sts. 107(123: 139) sts.
Shape top
Dec row K1, [K4(5: 6), K2 tog] 8 times, K4, K2 tog, K4, [K2 tog, K4(5: 6)] 8 times. 90(106: 122) sts.
Work 5 rows straight.
Dec row K2 tog, K2(3: 4), [K2 tog, K3(4:

5)] 8 times, K6(5: 4), [K2 tog, K3(4: 5)] 8 times.
Work 5 rows straight.
Dec row K1, [K2 tog, K7(9: 11)] 8 times.
Work 3 rows straight.
Dec row K1, [K2 tog, K6(8: 10)] 8 times.
Work 3 rows straight.
Dec row K1, [K2 tog, K5(7: 9)] 8 times.
Cont in this way, dec 8 sts as set on every 4th row until 17 sts rem.
Work 3 rows straight.
Dec row K1, [K2 tog] to end.
Break off yarn, thread end through rem sts, pull up and secure. Join seam.
With 3mm (No 11/US 2) needles and Red, cast on 3 sts.
Inc row (wrong side) [K1, P1] in first st, [K1, P1, K1] in next st, [K1, P1] in last st.
Beg with a K row, work 2 rows in st st.
Change to lurex and work 2 rows.
Change to Red and work 2 rows.
Dec row [K2 tog] 3 times, K1.
Dec row [P2 tog] twice.
Cast off. Run a gathering thread around edge, draw up to form bobble and secure. Make 5 more the same, then 6 more using Turquoise instead of Red and one more using Red instead of lurex and lurex instead of Red.
With crochet hook and using Pink and lurex together, make a chain approximately 75 (80: 85)cm/29½ (31½: 33½) in long. Attach one end of chain above rib on right ear point, wind around hat to top and stitch in place. Cut 2 stars out of felt and attach to top of hat. Sew on knitted and gold balls and buttons as desired. Glue on plastic stars. Sew on tiny dolls and embroider wings with lurex and daisy stitch.

Jester Hat and Gloves

See Page 20

MATERIALS

Hat 1 × 50g ball of Hayfield Grampian 4 ply in each of 3 colours (A, B and C).
Gloves Small amount of Hayfield Grampian 4 ply in each of 3 colours (A, B and C).
Pair each of 2¾mm (No 12/US 1) and 3¼mm (No 10/US 3) knitting needles.

MEASUREMENTS

To fit age
1–2(3–4) years

Hat

With 2¾mm (No 12/US 1) needles and A, cast on 116(124) sts.
Work 8cm/3in in K1, P1 rib.
Change to 3¼mm (No 10/US 3) needles.
Work in patt as follows:
1st row (right side) With B, K58(62), with

TENSION

28 sts and 36 rows to 10cm/4in square over st st on 3¼mm (No 10/US 3) needles.

ABBREVIATIONS

See page 41.

NOTE

When working in pattern, use separate ball for each coloured area and twist yarns together on wrong side at joins to avoid holes.

C, K58(62).
2nd row With C, P58(62), with B, P58(62).
Rep last 2 rows until work measures 18(20)cm/7(8)in from beg, ending with a wrong side row.
Shape points
Next row With B, K58(62), turn.

Work in B on this set of sts only. Cont in st st, dec one st at each end of 4th row, then on 2 foll 8th rows.
Now dec one st at each end of every foll 4th row until 28(30) sts rem, then on every foll alt row until 4 sts rem, ending with a P row. Break off yarn, thread end through rem sts, pull up and secure.
With right side facing, return to rem sts. Work in C on rem sts, K to end. Complete to match first side.
Join back seam to beginning of point shapings, then join seam of each point.
With A, make 2 pompons and attach one to end of each point.

Gloves

Right Hand

With 2¾mm (No 12/US 1) needles and A, cast on 36(40) sts.
Work 20 rows in K1, P1 rib, inc 5(6) sts evenly across last row. 41(46) sts.

Change to 3¼mm (No 10/US 3) needles and B.
Beg with a K row, work 10(12) rows in st st. **
Shape for thumb
Next row K17(19)B, 9(10)C, turn.
Cont in C only.
Next row Cast on 2 sts, P11(12), turn and cast on 2 sts.
Work 12(14) rows in st st on these 13(14) sts only.
Next row K1(0), [K2 tog] to end.
Next row P1, [P2 tog] to end. 4 sts.
Break off yarn, thread end through rem sts, pull up and secure. Join seam.
With right side facing and B, pick up and K3 sts from base of thumb, then K last 15(17) sts. 35(39) sts.
***Work a further 9(11) rows in st st across all sts.
Divide for fingers
Join in C.
Next row K23(25), turn.
Next row Cast on 1 st, P11(12), turn and cast on 1 st.

Work 16(18) rows in st st on these 12(13) sts only for first finger.
Next row K0(1), [K2 tog] to end.
Next row P0(1), [P2 tog] to end. 3(4) sts.
Break off yarn, thread end through rem sts, pull up and secure. Join seam.
With right side facing rejoin yarn to base of first finger, pick up and K2 sts from base of first finger, K4, turn.
Next row Cast on 1 st, P11(12), turn and cast on 1 st.
Work 18(20) rows in st st on these 12(13) sts only for second finger.
Complete as given for first finger.
With right side facing rejoin yarn to base of second finger, pick up and K2 sts from base of second finger, K4(5), turn.
Next row Cast on 1 st, P11(12), turn and cast on 1 st.
Work 16(18) rows in st st on these 12(13) sts only for third finger.
Complete as given for first finger.
With right side facing rejoin yarn to base of third finger, pick up and K2 sts from base of third finger, K4(5). Work 13(15)

rows in st st on rem 11(12) sts for fourth finger.
Next row K1(0), [K2 tog] to end.
Next row [P2 tog] to end. 3 sts.
Break off yarn, thread end through rem sts, pull up and secure. Join finger and side seam.

Left Hand
Work as given for Right Hand to **.
Shape for thumb
Next row K15(17)B, 9(10)C, turn.
Cont in C only.
Next row Cast on 2 sts, P11(12), turn and cast on 2 sts.
Work 12(14) rows in st st on these 13(14) sts only.
Next row K1(0), [K2 tog] to end.
Next row P1, [P2 tog] to end. 4 sts.
Break off yarn, thread end through rem sts, pull up and secure. Join seam.
With right side facing and B, pick up and K3 sts from base of thumb, then K last 17(19) sts. 35(39) sts. Complete as given for Right Hand from *** to end.

Segment Hat

See Page 21

MATERIALS
1 × 50g ball of Hayfield Silky Cotton DK in each of 3 colours (A, B and C). Pair of 4mm (No 8/US 5) knitting needles. Medium-size crochet hook.

MEASUREMENTS
To fit age
1–2(3–4) years

TENSION
22 sts and 28 rows to 10cm/4in square over st st on 4mm (No 8/US 5) needles.

ABBREVIATIONS
See page 41.

NOTE
When working segment pattern, use separate small balls of A and B for each coloured area and twist yarns together on wrong side at joins to avoid holes.

To Make
With 4mm (No 8/US 5) needles and C, cast on 116(123) sts.
Beg with a K row, work 7cm/2¾in in st st for brim, ending with a K row.
Dec row P2 tog, [P4, P2 tog] to last 0(1) st, P0(1). 96(102) sts.
Work in segment patt as follows:

1st row (right side) [K16(17)A, 16(17)B] 3 times.
2nd row [P16(17)B, 16(17)A] 3 times.
Rep last 2 rows 7(11) times more.
Shape top
Dec row [With A, sl 1, K1, psso, K12(13), K2 tog, with B, sl 1, K1, psso, K12(13), K2 tog] 3 times.

Keeping colours correct, work 3 rows.
Dec row [With A, sl 1, K1, psso, K10(11), K2 tog, with B, sl 1, K1, psso, K10(11), K2 tog] 3 times.
Keeping colours correct, work 3 rows.
Dec row [With A, sl 1, K1, psso, K8(9), K2 tog, with B, sl 1, K1, psso, K8(9), K2 tog] 3 times.
Cont in this way, dec 12 sts as set on every 4th row until 24(30) sts rem.
Keeping colours correct, work 3 rows.
Dec row [With A, sl 1, K1, psso, K2(3) tog, with B, sl 1, K1, psso, K2(3) tog] 3 times. 12 sts.
Break off yarns, thread one end through rem sts, pull up and secure. Join seam, reversing seam on brim. With crochet hook, right side facing and using two strands of C together, work vertical lines in chain st along joins of segments. With 4mm (No 8/US 5) needles and C, cast on 5 sts for stalk. K 5 rows. Cast off. Fold stalk in half lengthwise and join seam all round. Attach to top of hat. Roll up brim.

Clown Hat, Mittens and Slippers

See Page
22

MATERIALS
2×50g balls of Hayfield Grampian DK in each of Turquoise (A) and Yellow (B)
Small amount of same in Red.
Pair of 3¼mm (No 10/US 3) knitting needles.
Small amount of wadding.

MEASUREMENTS
To fit age
   1(2) years

TENSION
28 sts and 36 rows to 10cm/4in square over st st on 3¼mm (No 10/US 3) needles.

ABBREVIATIONS
See page 41.

NOTE
When working with 2 colours, twist yarns together on wrong side (knit side on brim, purl side on main part) at joins to avoid holes.

Hat

With 3¼mm (No 10/US 3) needles cast on 62(67) sts with B, then 62 (67) sts with A. 124(134) sts.
Work brim as follows:
1st row (wrong side) K62(67)A, 62(67)B.
2nd row P62(67)B, 62(67)A.
Rep last 2 rows until work measures 9cm/4½in from beg, ending with a wrong side row.
Dec row With B, *[P3, P2 tog, P1] 10(11) times, P2(1)*; with A rep from * to * once. 104(112) sts.
Work main part as follows:
1st row (right side) K52(56)A, 52(56)B.
2nd row P52(56)B, 52(56)A.
Rep last 2 rows 9(11) times more.
Shape top
Dec row With A, K2, [K2 tog tbl, K20(22), K2 tog, K1] twice, with B, [K1, K2 tog tbl, K20(22), K2 tog] twice, K2.
Next row P48(52)B, 48(52)A.
Next row K48(52)A, 48(52)B.
Next row P48(52)B, 48(52)A.
Rep last 2 rows twice more.
Dec row With A, K2, [K2 tog tbl, K18(20), K2 tog, K1] twice, with B, [K1, K2 tog tbl, K18(20), K2 tog] twice, K2.
Next row P44(48)B, 44(48)A.
Next row K44(48)A, 44(48)B.
Next row P44(48)B, 44(48)A.

Rep last 2 rows twice more.
Dec row With A, K2, [K2 tog tbl, K16(18), K2 tog, K1] twice, with B, [K1, K2 tog tbl, K16(18), K2 tog] twice, K2.
Keeping colours correct, cont in this way, dec 8 sts as set on foll 8th row and 2(3) foll 4th rows, then on every alt row until 40 sts rem, ending with a dec row.
Dec row With B, P2, [P2 tog, P4, P2 tog tbl, P1] twice, with A, [P1, P2 tog, P4, P2 tog tbl] twice, P2.
Dec row With A, K2, [K2 tog tbl, K2, K2 tog, K1] twice, with B, [K1, K2 tog tbl, K2, K2 tog] twice, K2.
Dec row With B, P2, [P2 tog, P2 tog tbl, P1] twice, with A, [P1, P2 tog, P2 tog tbl] twice, P2.
Dec row With A, [K2 tog] 4 times, with B, [K2 tog] 4 times.
Break off yarns, thread one end through rem sts, pull up and secure.
Join seam, reversing seam on brim. Allow brim to roll back, enclosing wadding. Catch down brim lightly. With Red, make 2 pompons and attach to hat as shown on photograph.

Mittens

(Not shown on photograph)

Right Hand
With 3¼mm (No 10/US 3) needles and A, cast on 28(32) sts.
Work 4cm/1½in in K1, P1 rib, inc one st at centre of last row on **1st** size only. 29(32) sts. Beg with a K row, work 4 rows in st st.
Shape for thumb
Inc row K15(16), m1, K1(2), m1, K13(14).
P 1 row.
Inc row K15(16), m1, K3(4), m1, K13(14).
P 1 row.
Inc row K15(16), m1, K5(6), m1, K13(14).
P 1 row.
Inc row K15(16), m1, K7(8), m1, K13(14). 37(40)sts.
P1 row.
Next row K24(26), turn.
** **Next row** Cast on 1 st, P10(11), turn and cast on 1 st.
Work 5(7) rows in st st on these 11(12) sts only.
Dec row P1(0), [P2 tog] to end. 6 sts.
Break off yarn, thread end through rem sts, pull up and secure. Join seam.
With right side facing, rejoin yarn to base of thumb, pick up and K3 sts from base of thumb, K rem sts. 31(33) sts. Work 11(15) rows in st st.
Dec row K1, [K2 tog tbl, K10(11), K2 tog, K1] twice.
P 1 row.

Dec row K1, [K2 tog tbl, K8(9), K2 tog, K1] twice.
P 1 row. Cast off. Join seam. With Red, make 2 pompons and attach to top of mitten.

Left Hand
With 3¼mm (No 10/US 3) needles and B, cast on 28(32) sts.
Work 4cm/1½in in K1, P1 rib, inc one st at centre of last row on **1st** size only. 29(32) sts. Beg with a K row, work 4 rows in st st.
Shape for thumb
Inc row K13(14), m1, K1(2), m1, K15(16).
P 1 row.
Inc row K13(14), m1, K3(4), m1, K15(16).
P 1 row.
Inc row K13(14), m1, K5(6), m1, K15(16).
P 1 row.
Inc row K13(14), m1, K7(8), m1, K15(16). 37(40) sts.
P 1 row.
Next row K22(24), turn.
Complete as given for Right Hand from ** to end.

Slippers

With 3¼mm (No 10/US 3) needles and A, cast on 18(22) sts.
Work in garter st (every row K) throughout, inc one st at each end of every alt row until there are 32(38) sts. Change to B. Dec one st at each end of next and every alt row until 18(22) sts rem.
Next row Cast on 7(8) sts for heel, K to end. 25(30) sts.
Inc one st at end of 6(7) foll alt rows. 31(37) sts. K1 row.
Next row Cast off knitwise 17(20) sts, K to last st, inc in last st.
K6(8) rows on these 15(18) sts.
Change to A.
K 6(8) rows.
Next row K2 tog, K to end, turn and cast on 17(20) sts. 31(37) sts.
Dec one st at beg of 6(7) foll alt rows. 25(30) sts. K 1 row.
Cast off knitwise.
Join back heel seam. Fold slipper along row just below cast on sts for heel and with right sides together, join seam all round, easing in fullness at toes and sewing the 7(8) cast on sts and last 7(8) sts of cast off edge to sole. Turn to right side. With Red, make 1 pompon and attach to slipper as shown on photograph.
Make one more.

Floppy Velvet Hat

See Page 23

MATERIALS
1×50g ball of Hayfield Crushed Velvet.
Pair of 3¾mm (No 9/US 4) knitting needles.
Medium-size crochet hook.

MEASUREMENTS
To fit age
1–2(3–4) years

TENSION
21 sts and 31 rows to 10cm/4in square over st st on 3¾mm (No 9/US 4) needles.

ABBREVIATIONS
Ch = chain; **dc** = double crochet.
Also see page 41.

Main Part
With 3¾mm (No 9/US 4) needles, cast on 90(100) sts.
Beg with a K row, work 9(10)cm/3½(4)in in st st, ending with a P row.
Shape top
Dec row [K7(8), K2 tog] to end.
P 1 row.
Dec row [K6(7), K2 tog] to end.
P 1 row.
Dec row [K5(6), K2 tog] to end.
Cont in this way, dec 10 sts as set on every alt row until 20 sts rem.
P 1 row.
Dec row [K2 tog] to end.
P 1 row.
Dec row [K2 tog] to end.
Break off yarn, thread end through rem sts, pull up and secure.

Brim
With 3¾mm (No 9/US 4) needles and right side facing, pick up and K90(98) sts along cast on edge of main part. Beg with a P row, cont in st st, work 1 row.
Inc row K2(3), [m1, K2] to last 0(1) st, K0(1). 134(145) sts.
P 1 row.
Inc row K2, [m1, K6(7), m1, K6] to end.
Work 3 rows.
Inc row K2, [m1, K7(8), m1, K7] to end.
Work 3 rows.
Inc row K2, [m1, K8(9), m1, K8] to end.
Cont in this way, inc 22 sts as set on every 4th row until there are 244(255) sts.
Work 5 rows.
With crochet hook, work picot edging as follows:
Next row [1 dc in next 3 sts, 3 ch, 1 dc in first of 3 ch (picot made)] to last 1(0) st, 1 dc in last 1(0) st. Fasten off.

To Make Up
Join seam.

Velvet Hat

See Page 23

MATERIALS
1×50g ball of Hayfield Crushed Velvet.
Pair of 3¾mm (No 9/US 4) knitting needles.
Medium-size crochet hook.

MEASUREMENTS
To fit age
1–2 years

TENSION
21 sts and 31 rows to 10cm/4in square over st st on 3¾mm (No 9/US 4) needles.

ABBREVIATIONS
Ch = chain; **dc** = double crochet.
Also see page 41.

Main Part
With 3¾mm (No 9/US 4) needles cast on 90 sts.
Beg with a K row, work 9cm/3½in in st st, ending with a P row.
Shape top
Dec row [K8, K2 tog] to end.
P 1 row.
Dec row [K7, K2 tog] to end.
P 1 row.
Dec row [K6, K2 tog] to end.
Cont in this way, dec 9 sts as set on every alt row until 18 sts rem.
P 1 row.
Dec row [K2 tog] to end.
Break off yarn, thread end through rem sts, pull up and secure.

Brim
With 3¾mm (No 9/US 4) needles and right side facing, pick up and K90 sts along cast on edge of main part. Beg with a P row, cont in st st, work 1 row.
Inc row K6, [m1, K6] to end.
Work 3 rows.
Inc row K6, [m1, K7] to end.
Work 3 rows.
Inc row K6, [m1, K8] to end.
Work 3 rows.
Inc row K6, [m1, K9] to end. 146 sts.
Work 5 rows.
With crochet hook, work edging as follows:
Next row [1 dc in next 3 sts, 3 ch, 1 dc in first of 3 ch (picot made)] to last 2 sts, 1 dc in last 2 sts. Fasten off.

To Make Up
Join seam.

Crochet Bonnet

See Page
24

MATERIALS
1 × 50g ball of Hayfield Silky Cotton DK.
3.50mm crochet hook.

MEASUREMENTS
To fit age
1–2 years

TENSION
20 sts and 15 rows to 10cm/4in square over pattern on 3.50mm hook.

ABBREVIATIONS
Ch = chain; dc = double crochet; ss = slip stitch; tr = treble.
Also see page 41.

To Make
With 3.50mm hook, make 4 ch, ss in first ch to form ring.
1st round Work 6 dc into ring, ss in first dc.

2nd round 2 dc in first dc, [1 dc in next dc, 2 dc in next dc] twice, 1 dc in last dc, ss in first dc.
3rd round 2 dc in first dc, [1 dc in next dc, 2 dc in next dc] 4 times, ss in first dc.
4th round 2 dc in first dc, [2 dc in next dc, 1 dc in next dc, 2 dc in next dc] 4 times, 2 dc in last dc, ss in first dc. 24 sts.
5th round 3 ch (counts as tr in first dc), 1 tr in last dc of last round, [miss next dc, 1 tr in next dc, 1 tr in missed dc] to end, ss in top of 3 ch.
6th round 2 dc in top of 3 ch, [2 dc in next tr, 1 dc in next tr, 2 dc in next tr] 7 times, 2 dc in next tr, 1 dc in last tr, ss in first dc. 40 sts.
7th round As 5th round.
8th round 2 dc in top of 3 ch, [2 dc in next tr, 1 dc in each of next 2 tr, 2 dc in next tr] 9 times, 2 dc in next tr,1 dc in each of last 2 tr, ss in first dc. 60 sts.
9th round As 5th round.
10th round 2 dc in top of 3 ch, [2 dc in next tr, 1 dc in each of next 3 tr, 2 dc in next tr] 11 times, 2 dc in next tr, 1 dc in

each of last 3 tr, ss in first dc. 84 sts.
11th round As 5th round.
12th round 1 dc in top of 3 ch, [1 dc in next tr] to end, ss in first dc.
13th round 1 dc in back loop of first dc, [1 dc in back loop of next dc] to end, ss in first dc, turn.
1st row (wrong side) 3 ch (counts as tr in first dc), [miss next dc, 1 tr in next dc, 1 tr in missed dc] 36 times, 1 tr in next dc, turn. 74 sts.
2nd row 1 dc in first tr, [1 dc in next tr] 72 times, 1 dc in top of 3 ch, turn.
Rep these 2 rows 4 times more, do not turn after last row.
Ties and edgings round Make 51 ch for tie, turn, 1 dc in 2nd ch from hook, [1 dc in next ch] 49 times, now work 35 dc along lower edge of bonnet, make 51 ch for tie, turn, 1 dc in 2nd ch from hook, [1 dc in next ch] 49 times, 1 dc in first dc, [3 ch, ss in 3rd ch from hook (picot made), miss next dc, 1 dc in next dc] to end, ss in last dc. Fasten off.

Lace-trimmed Hat

See Page
24

MATERIALS
2 × 50g balls of Hayfield Silky Cotton DK.
Pair of 3¾mm (No 9/US 4) knitting needles.

MEASUREMENTS
To fit age
1(2–3: 4–5) years

TENSION
24 sts and 30 rows to 10cm/4in square over st st on 3¾mm (No 9/US 4) needles.

ABBREVIATIONS
See page 41.

Main Part
With 3¾mm (No 9/US 4) needles cast on 94(104: 114) sts.
Beg with a K row, work 9(10: 11)cm/3½(4: 4½)in in st st, ending with a P row and dec 3(4: 5) sts evenly across last row. 91(100:109) sts.
Shape top
Dec row K1, [K2 tog, K8(9: 10)] to end.
P 1 row.
Dec row K1, [K2 tog, K7(8: 9)] to end.
P 1 row.
Dec row K1, [K2 tog, K6(7: 8)] to end.
Cont in this way, dec 9 sts as set on every

alt row until 19 sts rem.
P 1 row.
Dec row K1, [K2 tog] to end.
Break off yarn, thread end through rem sts, pull up and secure.

Brim
With 3¾mm (No 9/US 4) needles and right side facing, pick up and K92(106: 113) sts evenly along cast on edge of main part. Beg with a P row, cont in st st, work 1 row.
Inc row K1, [m1, K6(7: 8), m1, K7(8: 8)] 7 times.

Work 2 rows straight.
Inc row [P8(9: 9), m1, P7(8: 9), m1] 7 times, P1.
Work 2 rows straight.
Inc row K1, [m1, K8(9: 10), m1, K9(10: 10)] 7 times.
Work 2 rows straight.
Inc row [P10(11: 11), m1, P9(10: 11), m1] 7 times, P1. 148(162: 169) sts.
K 1 row. Cast off purlwise.

Edging
With 3¾mm (No 9/US 4) needles cast on 4 sts.
1st row (wrong side) K2, yf, K2.
2nd row and 2 foll alt rows K.
3rd row K3, yf, K2.
5th row K2, yf, K2 tog, yf, K2.
7th row K3, yf, K2 tog, yf, K2.
8th row Cast off 4, K to end.
These 8 rows form patt. Cont in patt until edging fits around brim, ending with 8th row. Cast off. Sew edging to brim. Join seam.

Elephant Hat and Mittens

See Page
25

MATERIALS

1×50g ball of Hayfield Grampian DK in Blue (A), and small amount in each of Green, Pink, Yellow, Red and Grey.
Pair of 3¼mm (No 10/US 3) knitting needles.

MEASUREMENTS

To fit age
    1(2–3: 4–6) years

TENSION

28 sts and 36 rows to 10cm/4in square over st st on 3¼mm (No 10/US 3) needles.

ABBREVIATIONS

See page 41.

NOTE

Read Charts from right to left on K rows and from left to right on P rows. When working Fair Isle pattern, strand yarn not in use loosely across wrong side to keep fabric elastic. When working elephant motifs, use separate lengths of yarn for each coloured area and twist yarns together on wrong side at joins to avoid holes.

Hat

With 3¼mm (No 10/US 3) needles and A, cast on 147(163: 179) sts.
1st row (right side) K1, [P1, K1] to end.
2nd row P1, [K1, P1] to end.
Cont in rib, work 2 rows.
Dec row Rib 29(33: 37), P3 tog, K1, P3 tog tbl, rib 75(83: 91), P3 tog, K1, P3 tog tbl, rib 29(33: 37).
Rib 1 row.
Dec row Rib 27(31: 35), P3 tog, K1, P3 tog tbl, rib 71(79: 87), P3 tog, K1, P3 tog tbl, rib 27(31: 35).
Rib 1 row.
Dec row Rib 25(29: 33), P3 tog, K1, P3 tog tbl, rib 67(75: 83), P3 tog, K1, P3 tog tbl, rib 25(29: 33).
Cont in this way, dec 8 sts as set on every alt row until 107(123: 139) sts rem, ending with a wrong side row.
Next row K24(28: 32), yf, sl 1, yb, turn.
Next row Sl 1, P3, yb, sl 1, yf, turn.
Next row Sl 1, K5, yf, sl 1, yb, turn.
Next row Sl 1, P7, yb, sl 1, yf, turn.
Cont in this way, working 2(2: 3) sts more at end of every row until the row "Sl 1, P27(11: 31), yb, sl 1, yf, turn" has been worked, then working 3 sts more at end of every row until the row "Sl 1, P45(53: 61)" has been worked.
Next row K across all sts.
Next row P24(28: 32), yb, sl 1, yf, turn.
Next row Sl 1, K3, yf, sl 1, yb, turn.
Next row Sl 1, P5, yb, sl 1, yf, turn.
Next row Sl 1, K7, yf, sl 1, yb, turn.
Cont in this way, working 2(2: 3) sts more at end of every row until the row "Sl 1, K27(11: 31), yf, sl 1, yb, turn" has been worked, then working 3 sts more at end of every row until row "Sl 1, K45(53: 61)" has been worked. 107(123: 139) sts. Cont in st st across all sts, work 0(2: 4) rows. Now work 1st to 5th rows of Chart 1. Join in Red and work 2 rows.
Work from Chart 2 as follows:
1st row (right side) K1(4: 7) Red, K across 1st row of Chart 2, [K3(5: 7) Red, K across 1st row of Chart 2] 5 times, K1(4: 7) Red.
2nd row P1(4: 7) Red, P across 2nd row of Chart 2, [P3(5: 7) Red, P across 2nd row of Chart 2] 5 times, P1(4: 7) Red.
Cont working from Chart 2 as set, work a further 4(6: 8) rows.
Shape top
1st size only
Dec row Patt 14, [K2 tog tbl, K 3 tog, patt 13] to last 3 sts, patt 3.
Patt 5 rows straight.
Dec row With Red, K1, [K3, K2 tog] 8 times, K4, K2 tog, K4, [K2 tog, K3] 8 times, K1.
Now work 1st to 5th rows of Chart 1 as given for 2nd size.
2nd and 3rd sizes only
Dec row Patt (1: 2), K2 tog tbl, patt (15: 19), [K2 tog tbl, K3 tog, patt (15: 17)] to last (5: 6) sts, patt (1: 2), K3 tog, patt (1: 1).
Patt (4: 2) rows straight.
Now work 1st to 4th rows of Chart 1.
Dec row With Green, P1, [P(5: 6), P2 tog] 7 times, P(5: 7), [P2 tog, P(5: 6)] 7 times, P1.

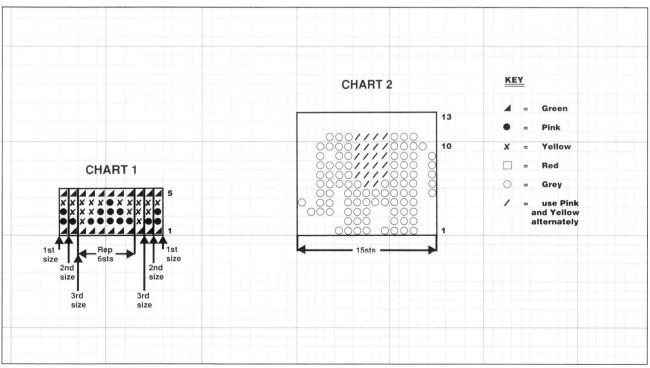

CHART 1

1st size
2nd size
3rd size
Rep 6sts
1st size
2nd size
3rd size

CHART 2

15sts

KEY

◢ = Green
● = Pink
✗ = Yellow
☐ = Red
○ = Grey
╱ = use Pink and Yellow alternately

continued overleaf

With A, work (2: 4) rows in st st.
All sizes
Cont in A only.
Dec row K1, [K2(3: 4), K2 tog] 8 times, K2, K2 tog, K1, K2 tog, K2, [K2 tog, K2(3: 4)] 8 times, K1.
Work 3(5: 5) rows in st st.
3rd size only
Dec row K1, [K2 tog, K9] 8 times.
P 1 row.
2nd and 3rd sizes only
Dec row K1, [K2 tog, K(7: 8)] 8 times.
P 1 row.
All sizes
Dec row K1, [K2 tog, K5(6: 7)] 8 times.
P 1 row.
Dec row K1, [K2 tog, K4(5: 6)] 8 times.
P 1 row.
Dec row K1, [K2 tog, K15(19: 23), K2 tog tbl, K1] twice.
P 1 row.
Dec row K1, [K2 tog, K13(17: 21), K2 tog tbl, K1] twice.
P 1 row.
Dec row K1, [K2 tog, K11(15: 19), K2 tog tbl, K1] twice.
Cont in this way, dec 4 sts as set on every alt row until 9 sts rem, ending with a wrong side row.
Dec row K1, [K3 tog, K1] twice.
Break off yarn, thread end through rem sts, pull up and secure. Join seam.

Mittens

Right hand
With 3¼mm (No 10/US 3) needles and Red, cast on 35(39: 43) sts.
1st row K1, [P1, K1] to end.

2nd row P1, [K1, P1] to end.
Beg with a K row, work in st st and patt from Chart 1 until 5th row of Chart 1 has been worked. Change to A and work 2(4: 6) rows in st st, then rep 1st and 2nd rows 6(7: 8) times, dec 2(1: 0) sts evenly across last row. 33(38: 43) sts. Change to Red. Beg with a K row (thus reversing fabric), work 0(2: 2) rows in st st. **
Shape for thumb
Next row K17(19: 21), m1, K1(2: 3), m1, K15(17: 19).
Work 1(1: 3) rows in st st. Turn Chart 2 upside down and work from it as follows:
Next row K1(2: 3) Red, K across 11th row of Chart 2, with Red, K1(2:3), m1, K3(4: 5), m1, K0(1: 2), K across 11th row of Chart 2, K0(1: 2) Red.
Next row P0(1: 2) Red, P across 10th row of Chart 2, P6(9: 12) Red, P across 10th row of Chart 2, P1(2: 3) Red.
Cont in this way, inc 2 sts as set on next and every foll alt row until there are 43(48: 53) sts, ending with a P row, **at the same time**, working 9th to 4th rows of Chart 2.
Next row Patt 28(31: 34), turn.
***Next row** With Red, cast on 1 st, P12(13: 14), turn and cast on 1 st.
Cont in Red and st st on these 13(14: 15) sts only, work 6(10: 12) rows.
Dec row [K2 tog] twice, [K3 tog] 1(2: 3) times, [K2 tog] 3(2: 1) times.
Break off yarn, thread end through rem sts, pull up and secure. Join seam.
With right side facing, rejoin Red yarn to base of thumb, pick up and K3 sts from base of thumb, patt rem sts. 35(39: 43) sts.
Work a further 2 rows in patt. With Red, work 2(4: 6) rows in st st. Now turn Chart

1 upside down and work 5th to 1st rows.
Cont in A only, work 0(4: 6) rows in st st.
Dec row K1, [sl 1, K1, psso, K12(14: 16), K2 tog, K1] twice.
Work 3 rows in st st.
Dec row K1, [sl 1, K1, psso, K10(12: 14), K2 tog, K1] twice.
P 1 row.
Dec row K1, [sl 1, K1, psso, K8(10: 12), K2 tog, K1] twice.
Dec row P1, [P2 tog, P6(8:10), P2 tog tbl, P1] twice.
Dec row K1, [sl 1, K1, psso, K4(6: 8), K2 tog, K1] twice.
Dec row P1, [P2 tog, P2(4: 6), P2 tog tbl, P1] twice.
Cast off. Join seam reversing seam on cuff. Turn back cuff.

Left Hand
Work as given for Right Hand to **.
Shape for thumb
Next row K15(17: 19), m1, K1(2: 3), K17(19: 21).
Work 1(1: 3) rows in st st. Turn Chart 2 upside down and work from it as follows:
Next row K0(1: 2) Red, K across 11th row of Chart 2, with Red, K0(1: 2), m1, K3(4: 5), m1, K1(2: 3), K across 11th row of Chart 2, K1(2: 3) Red.
Next row P1(2: 3) Red, P across 10th row of Chart 2, P6(9: 12) Red, P across 10th row of Chart 2, P0(1: 2) Red.
Cont in this way, inc 2 sts as set on next and every foll alt row until there are 43(48: 53) sts, ending with a P row, **at the same time**, working 9th to 4th rows of Chart 2.
Next row Patt 26(29: 32), turn.
Complete as given for Right Hand from *** to end.

Plain "Wee Willie Winkie" Hat, Mittens and Slippers

See Page 26

MATERIALS
Hat 2 × 50g balls of Hayfield Grampian DK.
Pair each of 3¼mm (No 10/US 3) and 4mm (No 8/US 5) knitting needles.

Mittens and Slippers 1 × 50g ball of Hayfield Grampian DK.
Pair each of 3¼mm (No 10/US 3) and 3¾mm (No 9/US 4) knitting needles.
Medium-size crochet hook.

MEASUREMENTS
To fit age
1–2(3–4) years

TENSION
22 sts and 28 rows to 10cm/4in square over st st on 4mm (No 8/US 5) needles.
24 sts and 30 rows to 10cm/4in square over st st on 3¾mm (No 9/US 4) needles.

ABBREVIATIONS
See page 41.

Hat

With 3¼mm (No 10/US 3) needles cast on 96(108) sts.
Work 6cm/2¼in in K2, P2 rib.
Change to 4mm (No 8/US 5) needles.

Beg with a K row, cont in st st until work measures 12(14)cm/4¾(5½)in from beg, ending with a P row.
Shape top
Dec row [K22(25), K2 tog tbl, K2 tog, K22(25)] twice.

Work 3 rows straight.
Dec row [K21(24), K2 tog tbl, K2 tog, K21(24)] twice.
Work 3 rows straight.
Dec row [K20(23), K2 tog tbl, K2 tog, K20(23)] twice.
Cont in this way, dec 4 sts as set on every foll 4th row until 20 sts rem. Work 3 rows straight. Break off yarn, thread end through rem sts, pull up and secure. Join seam. Make a large pompon and attach to top.

Mittens

(Not shown on photograph)

Right Hand
With 3¼mm (No 10/US 3) needles cast on 30(36) sts. Work 10(12) rows in K1, P1 rib inc one st at centre of last row on **1st** size only. 31(36) sts.

Change to 3¾mm (No 9/US 4) needles.
2nd size only
Beg with a K row, work 2 rows in st st.
Both sizes **
Shape for thumb
Inc row K16(18), m1, K1(2), m1, K14(16).
P 1 row.
Inc row K16(18), m1, K3(4), m1, K14(16).
P 1 row.
Inc row K16(18), m1, K5(6), m1, K14(16).
Cont in this way, inc 2 sts as set on every alt row until there are 41(46) sts, ending with a P row.
Next row K27(30), turn.
***Next row** Cast on 1 st, P12(13), turn and cast on 1 st.
Work 8(12) rows in st st on these 13(14) sts only.
Next row [K2 tog] twice, [K3 tog] 1(2) times, [K2 tog] 3(2) times. 6 sts.
Break off yarn, thread end through rem sts, pull up and secure. Join seam.
With right side facing, rejoin yarn to base of thumb, pick up and K3(4) sts from base of thumb, then K rem sts. 33(38) sts.
Work 15(23) rows in st st.
Dec row K1, K2 tog tbl, K11(13), K2 tog, K1(2), K2 tog tbl, K11(13), K2 tog, K1.

P 1 row.
Dec row K1, K2 tog tbl, K9(11), K2 tog, K1(2), K2 tog tbl, K9(11), K2 tog, K1.
P 1 row. Cast off. Join seam.

Left Hand
Work as given for Right Hand to **.
Shape for thumb
Inc row K14(16), m1, K1(2), m1, K16(18).
P 1 row.
Inc row K14(16), m1, K3(4), m1, K16(18).
P 1 row.
Inc row K14(16), m1, K5(6), m1, K16(18).
Cont in this way, inc 2 sts as set on every alt row until there are 41(46) sts, ending with a P row.
Next row K25(28), turn.
Complete as given for Right Hand from *** to end. With crochet hook, make a chain cord approximately 80(90)cm/31½(35½)in long. Make 2 small pompons and attach one to each end of cord, then attach cord to mittens.

Slippers

With 3¼mm (No 10/US 3) needles cast on

22(26) sts.
Work in garter st throughout (every row K), inc one st at each end of every alt row until there are 38(44) sts.
Dec one st at each end of next and every alt row until 22(26) sts rem.
Next row Cast on 8(9) sts for heel, K to end. 30(35) sts.
Inc one st at end of 7(8) foll alt rows. 37(43) sts. K 1 row.
Next row Cast off knitwise 20(22) sts, K to last st, inc in last st.
K18(22) rows on these 18(22) sts.
Next row K2 tog, K to end, turn and cast on 20(22) sts. 37(43) sts.
Dec one st at beg of 7(8) foll alt rows. 30(35) sts. K 1 row. Cast off knitwise. Join back heel seam. Fold slipper along row just below cast on sts for heel and with right sides together, join seam all round, easing in fullness at toes and sewing 8(9) cast on sts for heel and last 8(9) sts of cast off edge to sole. Turn to right side.
Make 1 pompon and attach to slipper as shown on photograph.
Make one more.

African-style Hat

See Page 27

MATERIALS
1 × 50g ball of Hayfield Raw Cotton Classics DK in Black (M).
Small amount of same in each of Jade (A) and Brick (B).
Pair of 4mm (No 8/US 5) knitting needles. Medium-size crochet hook.

MEASUREMENTS
To fit age
    1–2 years

TENSION
22 sts and 28 rows to 10cm/4in square over st st on 4mm (No 8/US 5) needles.

ABBREVIATIONS
Ch = chain; dc = double crochet.
Also see page 41.

NOTE
Read Chart from right to left on K rows and from left to right on P rows. When working in pattern, strand M and A yarns when not in use loosely across wrong side over no more than 4 sts at a time to keep fabric elastic; use separate lengths of B yarn for each motif and twist yarns together on wrong side at joins to avoid holes.

Main Part
With 4mm (No 8/US 5) needles and M, cast on 109 sts.
Beg with a K row, work 2 rows in st st.
Cont in st st and patt from Chart until 17th

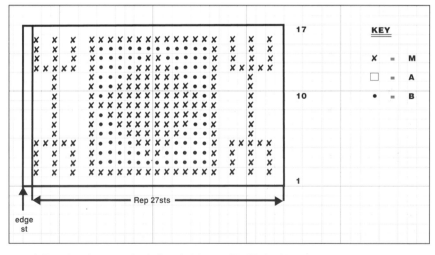

KEY

X = M

□ = A

• = B

Rep 27sts

edge st

row of Chart has been worked. Cont in M only, P 1 row.
Dec row [K8, K2 tog] to last 9 sts, K9. 99 sts.
Cast off purlwise.

Crown
With 4mm (No 8/US 5) needles and M, cast on 99 sts. K 1 row. P 1 row.
Dec row [K9, K2 tog] to end.
P 1 row.
Dec row [K8, K2 tog] to end.
P 1 row.
Dec row [K7, K2 tog] to end.
Cont in this way, dec 9 sts as set on every alt row until 18 sts rem. P1 row.
Dec row [K2 tog] to end.
Break off yarn, thread end through rem sts, pull up and secure.

To Make Up
Work crochet edging along cast on (lower) edge of main part as follows:
With crochet hook, right side facing and M, work 1 row of dc. DO NOT TURN. Now work 1 row of backward dc (dc worked from left to right). Fasten off. Work crochet edging along top edge of main part. Join seam of main part and crown. Sew crown in place, just below crochet edging.
Make stalk as follows: With crochet hook and M, make 5 ch.
1st row 1 dc in 2nd ch from hook, 1 dc in each of next 3 ch, turn.
2nd row 1 ch, miss first dc, 1 dc in each of next 3 dc, turn.
Rep 2nd row once. Fasten off.
Fold stalk in half lengthwise and join seam all round. Attach to top of crown.

Toy Hat

See Page
28

MATERIALS
1 × 50g ball of Hayfield Pure Wool Classics DK in Navy (A).
Small amount of same in each of Green (B), Blue (C), Yellow (D), Pink, Grey, Red and Brown.
Pair of 4mm (No 8/US 5) knitting needles.

MEASUREMENTS
To fit age
 2–4 years

TENSION
22 sts and 28 rows to 10cm/4in square over st st on 4mm (No 8/US 5) needles.

ABBREVIATIONS
See page 41.

NOTE
Read Chart from right to left on K rows and from left to right on P rows. When working in pattern or motifs, use separate small balls or lengths of yarn for each coloured area and twist yarns together on wrong side at joins to avoid holes.

Main Part
With 4mm (No 8/US 5) needles and A, cast on 96 sts.
Work 6cm/2¼in in st st, ending with a P row.
Work in patt as follows:
1st row (right side) [K16A, 16B] to end.
2nd row [P16B, 16A] to end.
These 2 rows form patt. Cont in patt until work measures 11cm/4½in from beg, ending with a wrong side row.
Shape top
Dec row [With A, sl 1, K1, psso, K12, K2 tog, with B, sl 1, K1, psso, K12, K2 tog] to end.
Next row [P14B, 14A] to end.
Next row [K14A, 14B] to end.
Next row [P14B, 14A] to end.
Dec row [With A, sl 1, K1, psso, K10, K2 tog, with B, sl 1, K1, psso, K10, K2 tog] to end.
Next row [P12B, 12A] to end.
Next row [K12A, 12B] to end.
Next row [P12B, 12A] to end.
Dec row [With A, sl 1, K1, psso, K8, K2 tog, with B, sl 1, K1, psso, K8, K2 tog] to end.
Keeping colours correct, cont in this way, dec 12 sts as set on every 4th row until 24 sts rem. Work 3 rows straight.
Dec row [With A, sl 1, K1, psso, K2 tog, with B, sl 1, K1, psso, K2 tog] to end.
Break off yarns, thread one end through rem sts, pull up and secure.

Brim
With 4mm (No 8/US 5) needles, A and wrong side facing, pick up and K96 sts evenly along cast on edge of main part.
P 1 row. K 1 row.
Inc row P6, [m1, P5] to end. 114 sts.
Beg with a K row, work in st st and patt from Chart until 17th row of Chart has been worked.
Dec row With A, P18, [P2 tog, P36] twice, P2 tog, P18. 111 sts.
Next row K3C, [5D, 5C] to last 8 sts, 5D, 3C.
Next row P2C, [2A, 3D, 2A, 3C] to last 9 sts, 2A, 3D, 2A, 2C.
Next row K1C, [4A, 1D, 4A, 1C] to end. Cont in A only.
Dec row P2, [P2 tog, P3] to last 4 sts, P2 tog, P2. 89 sts.
P 1 row for foldline. Beg with a P row, work 4 rows in st st for hem.
Cast off purlwise.

To Make Up
Join seam, reversing seam on brim. Fold hem to wrong side of brim at foldline and slip stitch in place. Turn back brim. With C, make a twisted cord approximately 5cm/2in long with a tassel at one end. Attach other end to top of hat.

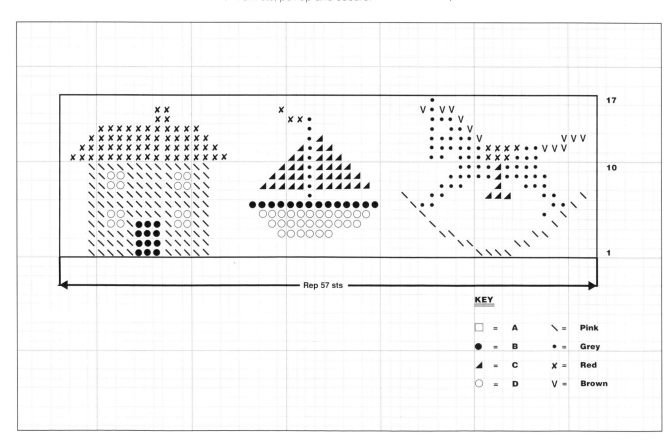

Rep 57 sts

KEY

□ = A		＼ =	Pink
● = B		• =	Grey
◢ = C		✗ =	Red
○ = D		V =	Brown

Peruvian Hat and Socks

See Page
29

MATERIALS
1 × 50g ball of Hayfield Grampian DK in each of 2 colours (A and B). Oddment of brightly coloured yarns for pompons.
Pair each of 3¾mm (No 9/US 4) and 4mm (No 8/US 5) knitting needles.
One 3¾mm (No 9/US 4) circular needle.

MEASUREMENTS
To fit age
    2 years

TENSION
22 sts and 28 rows to 10cm/4in square over st st on 4mm (No 8/US 5) needles.

ABBREVIATIONS
See page 41.

NOTE
Read Charts from right to left on K rows and from left to right on P rows. When working in pattern, strand yarn not in use loosely across wrong side to keep fabric elastic.

Hat

Ear Flaps (make 2)
With 4mm (No 8/US 5) needles and A, cast on 8 sts. P 1 row.
Beg with a K row and working in st st throughout, work 1st to 24th rows of Chart 1, **at the same time**, inc one st at each end of first 4 rows, then at each end of 4 foll alt rows. 24 sts. Leave these sts on a holder.

Main Part
With 4mm (No 8/US 5) needles and A, cast on 12 sts, K across sts of one ear flap, cast on 30 sts, K across sts of other ear flap, then cast on 12 sts. 102 sts. P 1 row B. Cont in st st and patt from Chart 2 as follows:
1st row (right side) Rep the 12 sts of 1st row of Chart 2 to last 6 sts, work first 6 sts.
2nd row Work last 6 sts of 2nd row of Chart 2, then rep the 12 sts to end.
Cont working from Chart 2 as set until 30th row of Chart 2 has been worked.
Shape top
Dec row With B, K2, *[K2 tog, K1] twice, K2 tog, K2; rep from * to end. 72 sts.
Work 1 row A and 1 row B. Now work 1st to 7th rows of Chart 2.
Dec row With B, [K1, K2 tog] to end. 48 sts.
Work 9th to 14th rows of Chart 2. Cont in A only, work 7 rows.
Dec row [K2 tog] to end.
Work 1 row.
Dec row [K2 tog] to end. 12 sts.
Break off yarn, thread end through rem sts, pull up and secure.

To Make Up
With 3¾mm (No 9/US 4) circular needle, A and right side facing, pick up and K1 st for each cast on st along cast on edges and 53 sts around each ear flap. 160 sts.
K 2 rows. Cast off knitwise.
Join seam. With A, make two 4cm/1½in long cords. Make 2 pompons with oddments of brightly coloured yarns and attach one to end of each cord. Attach other ends of cords to ear flaps.

Socks

With 3¾mm (No 9/US 4) needles and A, cast on 42 sts.
Work 6 rows in K1, P1 rib.
Change to 4mm (No 8/US 5) needles.
Beg with a K row and working in st st throughout, work in patt from Chart 2 as follows:
1st row (right side) Rep the 12 sts of 1st row of Chart 2 to last 6 sts, work first 6 sts.
2nd row Work last 6 sts of 2nd row of Chart 2, then rep the 12 sts to end.
Cont working from Chart 2 as set until 30th row of Chart 2 has been worked.
Work 1 row B, 1 row A and 1 row B, then work 1st to 6th rows of Chart 2 as before.
Shape heel
Next row With A, P5, P2 tog, P4 turn.
Change to B and work 9 rows on these 10 sts only.
Dec row P4, P2 tog, turn.
Next and foll alt row Sl 1, K to end.
Dec row P5, P2 tog, turn.
Dec row P6, P2 tog.
Leave rem 7 sts on a holder.
With wrong side facing, slip centre 20 sts onto a holder, rejoin A to rem 11 sts, P4, P2 tog, P5.
Change to B and work 8 rows on these 10

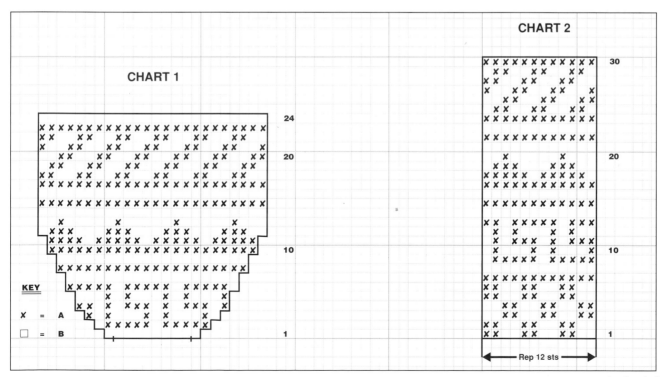

CHART 1

24

20

10

1

KEY

X = A

☐ = B

CHART 2

30

20

10

1

◄── Rep 12 sts ──►

continued overleaf

sts only.
Dec row K4, K2 tog tbl, turn.
Next and foll alt row Sl 1, P to end.
Dec row K5, K2 tog tbl, turn.
Dec row K6, K2 tog tbl, turn.
Next row Sl 1, P to end.
Change to A.
Shape instep
Next row K7, pick up and K8 sts along inside edge of heel, [K4, K2 tog, K4] twice across sts from holder, pick up and K8 sts along inside edge of heel, K7 sts from holder. 48 sts. P 1 row.
Dec row K13, K2 tog, K18, K2 tog tbl,

K13.
P 1 row.
Dec row K12, K2 tog, K18, K2 tog tbl, K12.
P 1 row.
Dec row K11, K2 tog, K18, K2 tog tbl, K11.
Cont in this way, dec 2 sts as set on every alt row until 38 sts rem.
Work 16 rows straight.
Change to B and P 1 row, dec one st at beg. 37 sts.
Shape toes
Dec row K1, [sl 1, K1, psso, K7] to end.

P 1 row.
Dec row K1, [sl 1, K1, psso, K6] to end.
P 1 row.
Dec row K1, [sl 1, K1, psso, K5] to end.
Cont in this way, dec 4 sts as set on every alt row until 17 sts rem.
Dec row [P2 tog] to last st, P1.
Break off yarn, thread end through rem sts, pull up and secure. Join seam. Make a pompon with oddments of brightly coloured yarns and attach to outside of sock, just below rib.
Make one more.

Mexican Dolls

See Page 29

MATERIALS
Oddment of Hayfield Grampian 4 ply in each of White and Light Pink.
Oddment of Hayfield Grampian DK in each of Black, Red, Blue, Green, Dark Pink and Yellow.
Pair each of 3mm (No 11/US 2) and 4mm (No 8/US 5) knitting needles.
Small amount of wadding.

MEASUREMENTS
Approximately 13cm/5in high.

ABBREVIATIONS
See page 41.

Boy Doll

Legs, Body and Head
With 3mm (No11/US 2) needles and White, cast on 5 sts for leg.
Inc row K1, [K twice in next st] 3 times, K1. 8 sts.
Beg with a P row, work 15 rows in st st. **
Leave these sts on a holder.
Work other leg as given for first leg to **.
Next row K8, then K8 sts from holder. 16 sts.
Work 15 rows in st st for body.
Change to Light Pink and work 10 rows for head.
Dec row [K2 tog] to end.
Break off yarn, thread end through rem sts, pull up and secure.

Arms (make 2)
With 3mm (No 11/US 2) needles and Light Pink, cast on 3 sts.
Inc row [K twice in next st] 3 times. 6 sts.
Beg with a P row, work 3 rows in st st.
Change to White and work a further 14 rows. Cast off.

Poncho
With 4mm (No 8/US 5) needles and Red, cast on 30 sts.
Beg with a P row, work in reverse st st and stripes of 4 rows Red, 2 rows Green, 4 rows Red, 2 rows Blue and 1 row Red.

Shape neck
Next row (wrong side) With Red, K11, cast off 8, K to end.
Next row With Red, P11, cast on 8, P to end.
Work 1 row Red, 2 rows Green, 4 rows Red, 2 rows Blue and 4 rows Red.
With Red, cast off purlwise.

Hat
With 3mm (No 11/US 2) needles and Black, cast on 44 sts. K 2 rows.
Dec row [K2 tog] to end.
Beg with a P row, work 7 rows in st st.
Dec row [K2 tog] to end.
Break off yarn, thread end through rem sts, pull up and secure.

To Make Up
Join leg seams, then back seam of body and head, leaving an opening.
Stuff lightly and close opening. Fold arms lengthwise and join long seam.
Stuff lightly, then run a gathering thread around cast off edge, pull up and secure. Sew arms to body. ****
Wind yarn round each wrist and neck, pull up tight and secure. Embroider facial features. With Black and straight stitches, embroider hair. Work ears at each side of head with Light Pink. Place poncho over body and fasten at sides. Join seam of hat. Place on head and secure in position.

Girl Doll

Legs, Body and Head
With 3mm (No 11/US 2) needles and Light Pink, cast on 5 sts for leg.
Inc row K1, [K twice in next st] 3 times, K1. 8 sts.
Beg with a P row, work 4 rows in st st.
Change to White and work a further 11 rows in st st. *** Leave these sts on a holder.
Work other leg as given for first leg to ***.
Complete as given for Legs, Body and Head of Boy Doll.

Arms (make 2)
Work as given for Arms of Boy Doll but

using Light Pink throughout.

Skirt
With 4mm (No 8/US 5) needles and Black, cast on 32 sts. K 2 rows.
Beg with a K row and working in st st throughout, work 1 row Red and 1 row Blue.
Next row [3 Blue, 1 Black] to end.
Next row [2 Black, 1 Blue, 1 Black] to end.
Work 2 rows Black and 1 row Dark Pink.
Cont in Black only, work 3 rows.
Dec row [K2 tog] to end.
Work 2 rows in K1, P1 rib. Cast off in rib.

Poncho
With 4mm (No 8/US 5) needles and Red, cast on 30 sts.
Beg with a P row, work in reverse st st and stripes of 2 rows Red, 2 rows Blue, 2 rows Green, 2 rows Dark Pink and 2 rows Yellow. Work a further 5 rows.
Shape neck
Next row (wrong side) With Green, K11, cast off 8, K to end.
Next row With Dark Pink, P11, cast on 8, P to end.
Work a further 15 rows. With Red, cast off purlwise.

Hat
Work as given for Hat of Boy Doll.

To Make Up
Work as given in To Make Up of Boy Doll to ****. Wind yarn round neck, pull up tightly and secure. Embroider facial features. Cut Black into six 15cm/6in lengths. Attach centre of all lengths to top of head. Plait lengths at each side and secure ends with Red bows. Join back seam of skirt and place on body, secure in position. Place poncho over body and fasten at sides. Join seam of hat. Place on head and secure in position.

Aran Hats

See Page
31

MATERIALS
2×50g balls of Hayfield Pure Wool Classics DK for each Hat.
Set of four in each of 3¼mm (No 10/US 3) and 4mm (No 8/US 5) double-pointed knitting needles. Cable needle.
Pair of 4mm (No 8/US 5) knitting needles and medium-size crochet hook for Hat with peak and ear flaps.

MEASUREMENTS
To fit age
   2–4 years

TENSION
22 sts and 28 rows to 10cm/4in square over st st on 4mm (No 8/US 5) needles.

ABBREVIATIONS
C6F = slip next 3 sts onto cable needle and leave at front, K3, then K3 from cable needle
C6B = slip next 3 sts onto cable needle and leave at back, K3, then K3 from cable needle
C4F = slip next 2 sts onto cable needle and leave at front, K2, then K2 from cable needle
C4B = slip next 2 sts onto cable needle and leave at back, K2, then K2 from cable needle
Cr3L = slip next 2 sts onto cable needle and leave at front, P1, then K2 from cable needle
Cr3R = slip next st onto cable needle and leave at back, K2, then P1 from cable needle
C5 = slip next 2 sts onto cable needle and leave at front, K2, P1, then K2 from cable needle
MB = [K1, P1] 3 times in next st, turn, P6, turn, K6, then pass 2nd, 3rd, 4th, 5th and 6th sts over first st
Also see page 41.

Pointed Hat

With set of four 3¼mm (No 10/US 3) needles cast on 106 sts.
Mark end of cast on row to indicate end of rounds.
Taking care not to twist the work, cont in rounds of K1, P1 rib for 6 rounds.
Inc round Inc in first st, [rib 4, inc in next st] to end. 128 sts.
Reset sts so that there are 32 sts on each of first and second needles and 64 sts on third needle.
Change to set of four 4mm (No 8/US 5) needles.
Work in patt as follows:
1st round [P1, K6, P7, C5, P7, K6] to end.
2nd round [P1, K6, P7, K2, P1, K2, P7, K6] to end.
3rd round [P1, C6F, P6, Cr3R, P1, Cr3L, P6, C6B] to end.
4th round [P1, K6, P6, K2, P3, K2, P6, K6] to end.
5th round [P1, K6, P5, Cr3R, P3, Cr3L, P5, K6] to end.
6th round [P1, K6, P5, K2, P5, K2, P5, K6] to end.
7th round [P1, K6, P4, Cr3R, P5, Cr3L, P4, K6] to end.
8th round [P1, K6, P4, K2, P7, K2, P4, K6] to end.
9th round [P1, C6B, P3, Cr3R, P7, Cr3L, P3, C6F] to end.
10th round [P1, K6, P3, K2, P9, K2, P3, K6] to end.
11th round [P1, K6, P2, Cr3R, P4, MB, P4, Cr3L, P2, K6] to end.
12th round [P1, K6, P2, K2, P11, K2, P2, K6] to end.
13th round [P1, K6, P2, Cr3L, P9, Cr3R, P2, K6] to end.
14th round As 10th round.
15th round [P1, C6F, P3, Cr3L, P7, Cr3R, P3, C6B] to end.
16th round As 8th round.
17th round [P1, K6, P4, Cr3L, P5, Cr3R, P4, K6] to end.
18th round As 6th round.
19th round [P1, K6, P5, Cr3L, P3, Cr3R, P5, K6] to end.
20th round As 4th round.
21st round [P1, C6B, P6, Cr3L, P1, Cr3R, P6, C6F] to end.
22nd round As 2nd round.
23rd and 24th rounds As 1st and 2nd rounds.
These 24 rounds form patt. Patt a further 20 rows. Break off yarn.
Reset sts on 3 needles by slipping last 16 sts from each needle onto beginning of following needle. Rejoin yarn to sts on first needle.
Shape top
Dec round [P1, sl 1, K1, psso, patt 59, K2 tog] twice.
Dec round [P1, sl 1, K1, psso, patt 57, K2 tog] twice.
Dec round [P1, sl 1, K1, psso, patt 55, K2 tog] twice.
Cont in this way, dec 4 sts as set on every round until 16 sts rem.
Break off yarn, thread end through rem sts, pull up and secure.
Make twisted cord approximately 4cm/1½ in long. Make a tassel and attach to one end of cord, attach other end of cord to top of hat. Fold over pointed top to one side and catch down in place.

Hat with Peak and Ear Flaps

Main Part
With set of four 4mm (No 8/US 5) needles cast on 128 sts (32 sts on each of first and second needle and 64 sts on third needle). Mark end of cast on row to indicate end of rounds. Taking care not to twist the work, cont in rounds.
Beg with a 10th round, work 29 rounds of patt as given for Pointed Hat.
Shape top
1st (dec) round [P1, C6F, P1, P2 tog, Cr3L, P7, Cr3R, P2 tog, P1, C6B] to end.
2nd round [P1, K6, P3, K2, P7, K2, P3, K6] to end.
3rd (dec) round [P1, K6, P1, P2 tog, Cr3L, P5, Cr3R, P2 tog, P1, K6] to end.
4th round [P1, K6, P3, K2, P5, K2, P3, K6] to end.
5th (dec) round [P1, K6, P1, P2 tog, Cr3L, P3, Cr3R, P2 tog, P1, K6] to end.
6th round [P1, K6, P3, K2, P3, K2, P3, K6] to end.
7th (dec) round [P1, C6B, P1, P2 tog, Cr3L, P1, Cr3R, P2 tog, P1, C6F] to end.
8th round [P1, K6, P3, K2, P1, K2, P3, K6] to end.
9th (dec) round [P1, K6, P1, P2 tog, C5, P2 tog, P1, K6] to end.
10th round [P1, K6, P2, K2, P1, K2, P2, K6] to end.
11th round [P1, K6, P2, C5, P2, K6] to end.
12th (dec) round * P1, [K2 tog, K1] twice, P2, K2, P1, K2, P2, [K1, K2 tog] twice; rep from * to end.
13th round [P1, C4F, P2, K2, P1, K2, P2, C4B] to end.
14th round [P1, K4, P2, K2, P1, K2, P2, K4] to end.
15th (dec) round * P1, [K2 tog] twice, P2, K1, sl 1, K2 tog, psso, K1, P2, [K2 tog] twice; rep from * to end.
16th round [P1, K2, P2, K3, P2, K2] to end.
17th (dec) round [P1, K2 tog, P2 tog, sl 1, K2 tog, psso, P2 tog, K2 tog] to end.
18th round [P1, K1] to end.
19th (dec) round [K2 tog] to end.
Break off yarn, thread end through rem sts, pull up and secure.

Peak
With 4mm (No 8/US 5) needles cast on 47 sts.
Foundation row (wrong side) [K1, P6], twice, K7, P5, K7, [P6, K1] twice.
Work in patt as follows:
1st row [P1, K6] twice, P7, C5, P7, [K6, P1] twice.
2nd row [K1, P6] twice, K7, P2, K1, P2, K7, [P6, K1] twice.
3rd row P1, C6B, P1, C6F, P6, Cr3R, P1, Cr3L, P6, C6B, P1, C6F, P1.
4th row [K1, P6] twice, K6, P2, K3, P2, K6, [P6, K1] twice.
5th row [P1, K6] twice, P5, Cr3R, P3, Cr3L, P5, [K6, P1] twice.
6th row [K1, P6] twice, K5, [P2, K5] twice, [P6, K1] twice.
These 6 rows set the patt. Cont in patt as set, work a further 6 rows.
Dec row Sl 1, K2 tog, psso, patt to last 3 sts, K3 tog.
Dec row P2 tog, patt to last 2 sts, P2 tog

continued overleaf

tbl.
Rep last 2 rows 5 times more. Cast off rem 11 sts.

Ear Flaps (make 2)
With 4mm (No 8/US 5) needles cast on 33 sts.
Foundation row (wrong side) K1, P6, K2, P2, K11, P2, K2, P6, K1.
Work in patt as follows:
1st row P1, K6, P2, Cr3L, P9, Cr3R, P2, K6, P1.
2nd row K1, P6, K3, P2, K9, P2, K3, P6, K1.
3rd row P1, C6F, P3, Cr3L, P7, Cr3R, P3, C6B, P1.
4th row K1, P6, K4, P2, K7, P2, K4, P6, K1.
5th row P1, K6, P4, Cr3L, P5, Cr3R, P4, K6, P1.
6th row K1, P6, K5, [P2, K5] twice, P6, K1.
These 6 rows set the patt. Cont in patt as set, work a further 20 rows.
Dec row P1, C6F, P1, P2 tog, Cr3L, P7,

Cr3R, P2 tog, P1, C6B, P1.
Next row K1, P6, K3, P2, K7, P2, K3, P6, K1.
Dec row P1, K6, P1, P2 tog, Cr3L, P5, Cr3R, P2 tog, P1, K6, P1.
Next row K1, P6, K3, P2, K5, P2, K3, P6, K1.
Dec row P1, K6, P1, P2 tog, Cr3L, P3, Cr3R, P2 tog, P1, K6, P1.
Next row K1, P6, K3, P2, K3, P2, K3, P6, K1.
Dec row P1, C6B, P1, P2 tog, Cr3L, P1, Cr3R, P2 tog, P1, C6F, P1.
Next row K1, P6, K3, P2, K1, P2, K3, P6, K1.
Dec row P1, K6, P1, P2 tog, C5, P2 tog, P1, K6, P1.
Next row K1, [P2 tog] 3 times, K2 tog, P2 tog, K1, P2 tog, K2 tog, [P2 tog] 3 times, K1.
Cast off rem 13 sts.

Peak Lining
With 4mm (No 8/US 5) needles cast on 32 sts. K 16 rows.

Dec row K2 tog, K to last 2 sts, K2 tog.
Rep last row until 8 sts rem. Cast off.

Ear Flap Linings (make 2)
With 4mm (No 8/US 5) needles cast on 12 sts. K 1 row.
Inc row K twice in first st, K to last st, K twice in last st.
Rep last 2 rows once more. 16 sts. Cont in garter st (every row K) until lining, when slightly stretched, measures same as ear flap. Cast off.

To Make Up
Line ear flaps and peak.
With crochet hook, work 2 rows of double crochet along cast on edge of main part and around ear flaps and peak, omitting cast on edges.
Sew peak to front of main part. Gather slightly cast on edge of ear flaps and sew to main part underneath edging.
Make tassel approximately 3cm/1¼in long and attach to top of hat.

Plain Fur-lined Hat

See Page
30

MATERIALS
2 × 50g balls of Hayfield Grampian DK.
Pair of 6½mm (No 3/US 10) knitting needles.
Medium-size crochet hook.
Approximately 60cm × 30cm/23½in × 12in piece of fur fabric for lining.

MEASUREMENTS
To fit age
2–4 years

TENSION
14 sts and 19 rows to 10cm/4in square over st st on 6½mm (No 3/US 10) needles using two strands of yarn together.

ABBREVIATIONS
See page 41.

Ear Flaps (make 2)
With 6½mm (No 3/US 10) needles and two strands of yarn together, cast on 5 sts.
Beg with a K row, work in st st, inc one st at each end of 2nd row and 3 foll rows. 13 sts. Work 21 rows straight. Leave these sts on a holder.

Peak
With 6½mm (No 3/US 10) needles and two strands of yarn together, cast on 20 sts.
Beg with a K row, work in st st, inc one st at each end of 2nd row and 3 foll rows. 28 sts. Work 9 rows straight. Leave these sts on a holder.

Crown
With 6½mm (No 3/US 10) needles and two strands of yarn together, cast on 6 sts, then K across sts of one ear flap, cast on 3 sts, K across peak sts, cast on 3 sts, K across sts of other ear flap, cast on 6 sts. 72 sts. Cont in st st for a further 10cm/4in, ending with a P row.

Shape top
Dec row [K7, K2 tog] to end.
P 1 row.
Dec row [K6, K2 tog] to end.
P 1 row.
Dec row [K5, K2 tog] to end.
Cont in this way, dec 8 sts as set on every alt row until 16 sts rem.
P 1 row.
Dec row [K2 tog] to end.
Break off yarn, thread end through rem sts, pull up and secure.

To Make Up
With crochet hook, right side facing and two strands of yarn together, work 1 row of double crochet along lower edge, including ear flaps and peak. Turn and work 1 more row of double crochet, working 2 double crochet together in corners at each side of ear flaps and peak. Fasten off.
Make 2 twisted cords approximately 25cm/10in long and attach one to each ear flap. Cut fur fabric to fit hat and join seams. Join seam of hat. Insert lining into hat and slip stitch in place.

Fur-lined Fair Isle Hat

See Page
30

MATERIALS
1 × 100g ball of Hayfield Grampian Chunky in each of Natural (A), Tobacco (B) and Black (C).
Small amount of same in each of Rust (D), Cream (E) and Blue (F). Hayfield Grampian DK used double can be substituted for colours D, E and F.
Pair of 6½mm (No 3/US 10) knitting needles.
Medium-size crochet hook.
Approximately 60cm × 30cm/23½in × 12in piece of fur fabric for lining.

MEASUREMENTS
To fit age
2–4 years

TENSION
14 sts and 19 rows to 10cm/4in square over st st on 6½mm (No 3/US 10) needles.

ABBREVIATIONS
See page 41.

NOTE
Read Charts from right to left on K rows and from left to right on P rows. When working in pattern, strand yarn not in use loosely across wrong side over no more than 3 sts at a time to keep fabric elastic.

Right Ear Flap
With 6½mm (No 3/US 10) needles and A, cast on 5 sts.
Beg with a K row and 1st row of Chart 1, work in st st and patt from Chart 1, inc one st at each end of 2nd row and 3 foll rows. 13 sts. Cont working from Chart 1 until 11th row of Chart 1 has been worked.
Now work 1st to 7th rows of Chart 2 as applicable. Leave these sts on a holder.

Left Ear Flap
Work as given for Right Ear Flap.

Peak
With 6½mm (No 3/US 10) needles and C, cast on 23 sts.
Beg with a K row and 1st row of Chart 3, work 5 rows in st st and patt from Chart 3, inc one st at each end of 2nd row and 3 foll rows. 31 sts.
Now work 1st to 7th rows of Chart 2 as applicable. Leave these sts on a holder.

Crown
With 6½mm (No 3/US 10) needles and A, cast on 7 sts, then K across Left Ear Flap sts, cast on 4 sts, K across Peak sts, cast on 4 sts, K across Right Ear Flap sts, cast on 7 sts. 79 sts. Cont in st st, work 1st to 10th rows of Chart 4, then work 1st to 7th rows of Chart 2 as applicable.

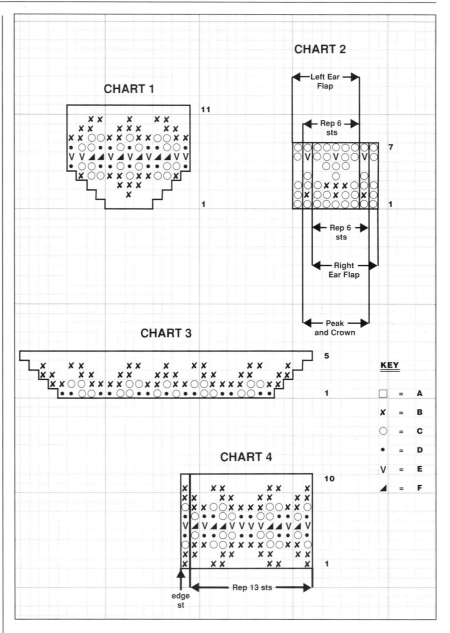

KEY
□ = A
✗ = B
○ = C
• = D
V = E
◢ = F

Shape top
Dec row With A, K7, [K2 tog, K7] to end. 71 sts.
Next row P1B, [6A, 1B] to end.
Dec row K2B, [with A, K1, K2 tog, K1, K3B] to last 6 sts, with A, K1, K2 tog, K1, K2B. 61 sts.
Next row P1B, [5D, 1B] to end.
Dec row K1B, [with D, K2, K2 tog, K1, K1B] to end. 51 sts.
Next row P2B, [2A, 3B] to last 4 sts, 2A, 2B.
Dec row K1B, [with A, K1, K2 tog, K1, K1B] to end. 41 sts.
P 1 row A.
Dec row With C, K2, [K2 tog, K1] to end. 28 sts.
Next row P1B, [2C, 1B] to end.

Dec row K1C, [with B, K2 tog, K1C] to end. 19 sts.
P 1 row C.
Dec row With C, K1, [K2 tog] to end. 10 sts. Break off yarn, thread end through rem sts, pull up and secure.

To Make Up
With crochet hook, right side facing and C, work 1 row of double crochet along lower edge including ear flaps and peak. Turn. Work 1 more row of double crochet, working 2 double crochet together in corners at each side of flaps and peak. Fasten off. Cut fur fabric lining to fit hat and join seams. Join seam of hat. Insert lining into hat and stitch in place.

Aran Scarf and Fingerless Gloves

See Page
32

MATERIALS

Scarf 3 × 50g balls of Hayfield Grampian 4 ply.
One 3¼mm (No 10/US 3) circular knitting needle.
Pair each of 2¾mm (No 12/US 1) and 3¼mm (No 10/US 3) knitting needles.
Cable needle.
Gloves 1 × 50g ball of Hayfield Grampian 4 ply.
Pair each of 2¾mm (No 12/US 1) and 3mm (No 11/US 2) knitting needles.

MEASUREMENTS

To fit age
    3 years

TENSION

38 sts and 40 rows to 10cm/4in square over pattern on 3¼mm (No 10/US 3) needles.
30 sts and 38 rows to 10cm/4in square over st st on 3mm (No 11/US 2) needles.

ABBREVIATIONS

C4B = slip next 2 sts onto cable needle and leave at back, K2, then K2 from cable needle
C4F = slip next 2 sts onto cable needle and leave at front, K2, then K2 from cable needle
Cr3L = slip next 2 sts onto cable needle and leave at front, P1, then K2 from cable needle
Cr3R = slip next st onto cable needle and leave at back, K2, then P1 from cable needle
Also see page 41.

Scarf

Panel A – worked over 20 sts.
1st row (right side) [P2, Cr3R] twice, [Cr3L, P2] twice.
2nd row K2, P2, K3, P2, K2, P2, K3, P2, K2.
3rd row P1, [Cr3R, P2] twice, Cr3L, P2, Cr3L, P1.
4th row K1, P2, K3, P2, K4, P2, K3, P2, K1.
5th row [Cr3R, P2] twice, pick up loop lying between st just worked and next st and work [K1, P1, K1] all into the back of it, turn, P3, turn, K3, turn, P3, turn, P3 tog, P1 then pass bobble st over first st, P1, Cr3L, P2, Cr3L.
6th row [P2, K3] twice, [K3, P2] twice.
7th row [Cr3L, P2] twice, [P2, Cr3R] twice.
8th row As 4th row.
9th row P1, [Cr3L, P2] twice, Cr3R, P2, Cr3R, P1.

10th row As 2nd row.
11th row [P2, Cr3L] twice, [Cr3R, P2] twice.
12th row [K3, P2] twice, [P2, K3] twice.
These 12 rows form patt.

Panel B – worked over 6 sts.
1st row (right side) P1, K4, P1.
2nd row K1, P4, K1.
3rd row P1, C4F, P1.
4th row As 2nd row.
These 4 rows form patt.

Panel C – worked over 10 sts.
1st row (right side) P1, K8, P1.
2nd row and 2 foll alt rows K1, P8, K1.
3rd row P1, C4B, C4F, P1.
5th row As 1st row.
7th row P1, C4F, C4B, P1.
8th row As 2nd row.
These 8 rows form patt.

Panel D – worked over 6 sts.
1st row (right side) P1, K4, P1.
2nd row K1, P4, K1.
3rd row P1, C4B, P1.
4th row As 2nd row.
These 4 rows form patt.

First side

With 3¼mm (No 10/US 3) needles cast on 21 sts.
1st row (wrong side) K1, work 12th row of Panel A.
2nd row Cast on 6 sts, work 3rd row of Panel D, work 1st row of Panel A, P1.
3rd row K1, work 2nd row of Panel A, work 4th row of Panel D.
4th row Cast on 10 sts, work 1st row of Panel C, work 1st row of Panel D, patt to last st, P1.
5th row K1, patt 20, work 2nd row of Panel D and Panel C.
6th row Cast on 6 sts, work 3rd row of Panel B, patt to last 3 sts, work 3 tog.
7th row Work 2 tog, patt to last 6 sts, work 4th row of Panel B.
8th row Cast on 20 sts, work 7th row of Panel A, work 1st row of Panel B, patt to last 2 sts, work 2 tog.
9th row Work 2 tog, patt to last 26 sts, work 2nd row of Panel B and 8th row of Panel A.
Cont in this way, casting on 6 sts for Panel D at beg of next row, 10 sts for Panel C at beg of foll alt row, 6 sts for Panel B at beg of foll alt row, then 20 sts for Panel A at beg of foll alt row, **at the same time**, dec one st at end of next row and at same edge on foll 2 rows, then 2 sts at same edge on next row and one st at same edge on foll 3 rows until there are 160 sts, ending with a wrong side row and 5th set of 6 cast on sts for Panel D.
Leave these sts on a spare needle.

Second side

With 3¼mm (No 10/US 3) needles cast on 21 sts.
1st row (right side) P1, work 1st row of Panel A.
2nd row Cast on 6 sts, work 4th row of Panel B and 2nd row of Panel A, K1.
3rd row P1, patt 20, work 1st row of Panel B.
4th row Cast on 10 sts, work 2nd row of Panel C and Panel B, patt to last st, K1.
5th row Work 3 tog, patt to last 10 sts, work 3rd row of Panel C.
6th row Cast on 6 sts, work 4th row of Panel D and Panel C, patt to last 2 sts, work 2 tog.
7th row Work 2 tog, patt to last 6 sts, work 1st row of Panel D.
8th row Cast on 20 sts, work 8th row of Panel A and 2nd row of Panel D, patt to last 2 sts, work 2 tog.
Cont in this way, dec one st at beg of next row and at same edge on 2 foll rows, then 2 sts at same edge on next row and one st at same edge on foll 3 rows, **at the same time**, casting on 6 sts for Panel B at beg of foll alt row, 10 sts for Panel C at beg of foll alt row, 6 sts for Panel D at beg of foll alt row, then 20 sts for Panel A at beg of foll alt row until there are 160 sts, ending with a wrong side row and 5th set of 6 cast on sts for Panel B.
Change to 3¼mm (No 10/US 3) circular needle. Work backwards and forwards.
Next row Work 2 tog, patt to end, cast on 10 sts for Panel C, patt across first side to last 2 sts, work 2 tog. 328 sts.
Cont in patt, dec one st at each end of next 3 rows, 2 sts at each end of next row, then one st at each end of foll 3 rows until 2 sts rem.
Work 2 tog and fasten off.

Edgings

With 2¾mm (No 12/US 1) needles and right side facing, pick up and K194 sts evenly along one short edge. Work 6 rows in K1, P1 rib, inc one st at each end of every alt row. Cast off in rib.
Work other short edge in same way.
With 2¾mm (No 12/US 1) needles and right side facing, pick up and K306 sts evenly along long edge omitting edgings. Work 6 rows in K1, P1 rib, inc one st at each end of every alt row. Cast off in rib.

To Make Up

Mitre all corners. Make 3 pompons and attach one to each corner.

Fingerless Gloves

With 2¾mm (No 12/US 1) needles cast on 39 sts.

1st row (right side) K1, [P1, K1] to end.
2nd row P1, [K1, P1] to end.
Rep last 2 rows until work measures 4cm/1½in from beg, ending with a 2nd row.
Change to 3mm (No 11/US 2) needles.
Beg with a K row, cont in st st, work 4 rows.

Shape for thumb
Inc row K19, m1, K1, m1, K19.
P 1 row.
Inc row K19, m1, K3, m1, K19.
P 1 row.
Inc row K19, m1, K5, m1, K19.
Cont in this way, inc 2 sts as set on every alt row until there are 49 sts.
P 1 row.
Next row K30, turn.
Next row Cast on 2, P13, turn and cast on 2 sts.
Work on these 15 sts only.
** Change to 2¾mm (No 12/US 1) needles.
Rep 1st and 2nd rows twice. Cast off in rib. Join seam. **
With right side facing, rejoin yarn to base of thumb and with 3mm (No 11/US 2) needles , pick up and K3 sts from base of thumb, K rem sts. 41 sts.
Work 11 rows.

Shape for fingers
Next row K26, turn.
Next row Cast on 1 st, P12, turn and cast on 1 st.
Work on these 13 sts only for first finger as given for thumb from ** to **.
With right side facing, rejoin yarn to base of first finger and with 3mm (No 11/US 2) needles, pick up and K2 sts from base of first finger, K5, turn.
Next row Cast on 1 st, P13, turn and cast on 1 st.
Work on these 14 sts only for second finger.
Change to 2¾mm (No 12/US 1) needles and work 4 rows in K1, P1 rib.
Cast off in rib. Join seam.
With right side facing, rejoin yarn to base of second finger and with 3mm (No 11/US 2) needles, pick up and K2 sts from base of second finger, K5, turn.
Next row Cast on 1 st, P6, P2 tog, P5, turn and cast on 1 st.
Work on these 13 sts only for third finger as given for thumb from ** to **.
With right side facing, rejoin yarn to base of third finger and with 3mm (No 11/US 2) needles, pick up and K2 sts from base of third finger, K5, turn, P12.
Work on these 12 sts for fourth finger.
Change to 2¾mm (No 12/US 1) needles and work 4 rows in K1, P1 rib. Cast off in rib. Join finger and side seam.
Make one more.

Fair Isle Triangle Scarf, Gloves and Socks

See Page 33

MATERIALS
Scarf 1×50g ball of Hayfield Grampian 4 ply in each of Navy (M) and Mustard (A).
Small amount of same in each of Olive (B), Red (C), Blue (D), Rust (E) and Lilac (F).
Gloves and socks 1×50g ball of Hayfield Grampian 4 ply in Navy (M).
Small amount of same in each of Mustard (A), Olive (B), Red (C), Blue (D), Rust (E) and Lilac (F).
Pair each of 2¾mm (No 12/US 1) and 3¼mm (No 10/US 3) knitting needles.
Set of four each of 2¾mm (No 12/US 1) and 3¼mm (No 10/US 3) double pointed knitting needles for socks.

MEASUREMENTS
To fit age
3–5 years

TENSION
30 sts and 34 rows to 10cm/4in square over Fair Isle pattern on 3¼mm (No 10/US 3) needles.

ABBREVIATIONS
See page 41.

NOTE
Read Chart from right to left on K rows and from left to right on P rows. When working in pattern, strand yarn not in use loosely across wrong side to keep fabric elastic.

Scarf

First Side
With 3¼mm (No 10/US 3) needles and M, cast on 25 sts. P 1 row.
Next row (right side) Cast on 8 sts, K last 8 sts of 1st row of Chart, then K the 24 sts, K first st.
Next row P last st of 2nd row of Chart, P the 24 sts, then P first 8 sts.
Next row Cast on 8 sts, K last 16 sts of 3rd row of Chart, then K the 24 sts, K first st.
Next row P last st of 4th row of Chart, P the 24 sts, then P first 16 sts.
Cont in this way, casting on and working into patt 8 sts at beg of next and every foll alt row, **at the same time**, dec one st at end of next row and at same edge on every foll row until there are 119 sts, ending with a wrong side row and 15th set of 8 cast on sts. Leave these sts on a spare needle.

Second Side
With 3¼mm (No 10/US 3) needles and M, cast on 25 sts.
Next row (right side) K the 24 sts of 1st row of Chart, then K first st.
Next row Cast on 8 sts, P last 9 sts of 2nd row of Chart, then P the 24 sts.
Next row K the 24 sts of 3rd row of Chart, then K first 9 sts.
Next row Cast on 8 sts, P last 17 sts of 4th row of Chart, then P the 24 sts.
Cont in this way, casting on and working into patt 8 sts at beg of every alt row, **at the same time**, dec one st at beg of next row and at same edge on every row until there are 119 sts, ending with a wrong side row and 15th set of 8 cast on sts.
Next row Work 2 tog, patt to end, cast on 23 sts, then patt across sts of first side to last 2 sts, work 2 tog. 259 sts.
Cont in patt across all sts, dec one st at each end of every row until 3 sts rem.
Work 3 tog and fasten off.

Edgings
With 2¾mm (No 12/US 1) needles, M and right side facing, pick up and K194 sts evenly along one short edge. Work 6 rows in K1, P1 rib, inc one st at each end of every alt row. Cast off in rib. Work other short edge in same way.
With 2¾mm (No 12/US 1) needles, M and right side facing, pick up and K306 sts evenly along long edge, omitting edgings of short edges. Work 6 rows in K1, P1 rib, inc one st at each end of every alt row.
Cast off in rib. Join edging seams at points.

Gloves

Right Hand
With 2¾mm (No 12/US 1) needles and M, cast on 40 sts. Work 20 rows in K1, P1 rib, inc 9 sts evenly across last row. 49 sts.
Change to 3¼mm (No 10/US 3) needles.
Next row K the 24 sts of 5th row of Chart twice, then K first st.
Next row P last st of 6th row of Chart, then P the 24 sts twice.
Work a further 8 rows in patt from Chart as set. **
Shape for thumb
Next row K first 21 sts of 15th row of Chart, with M, K10, turn.
Next row With M, cast on 2 sts, P12, turn and cast on 2 sts.
Work 14 rows in st st and M on these 14 sts only.
Next row [K2 tog] to end.
Next row P1, [P2 tog] to end. 4 sts.
Break off yarn, thread end through rem sts, pull up and secure. Join seam.
With right side facing, rejoin M yarn to base of thumb, pick up and K3 sts from

continued overleaf

base of thumb, then K last 17 sts of 15th
row of Chart, K first st. 42 sts.
***Next row P last st of 16th row of Chart,
then P first 20 sts, P last 21 sts.
Next row K first 21 sts of 17th row of
Chart, K last 20 sts, then K first st.
Work a further 8 rows in patt from Chart
as set. Cont in M only.
Next row P6, P2 tog, P12, P2 tog, P7, P2
tog, P11. 39 sts.
Divide for fingers
Next row K25, turn.
Next row Cast on 1 st, P12, turn and cast
on 1 st.
Work 18 rows in st st on these 13 sts only
for first finger.
Next row K1, [K2 tog] to end.
Next row P1, [P2 tog] to end.
Break off yarn, thread end through rem
sts, pull up and secure. Join seam.
With right side facing, rejoin yarn to base
of first finger, pick up and K2 sts from
base of first finger, K4, turn.
Next row Cast on 1 st, P12, turn and cast
on 1 st.
Work 20 rows in st st on these 13 sts only
for second finger. Complete as given for
first finger.
With right side facing, rejoin yarn to base
of second finger, pick up and K2 sts from
base of second finger, K5, turn.
Next row Cast on 1 st, P12, turn and cast

on 1 st.
Work 18 rows in st st on these 13 sts only
for third finger. Complete as given for first
finger.
With right side facing, rejoin yarn to base
of third finger, pick up and K2 sts from
base of third finger, K5. Work 15 rows in
st st on rem 12 sts for fourth finger.
Next row [K2 tog] to end.
Next row [P2 tog] to end.
Break off yarn, thread end through rem
sts, pull up and secure. Join finger and
side seam.

Left Hand
Work as given for Right Hand to **.
Shape for thumb
Next row K first 18 sts of 15th row of
Chart, with M, K10, turn.
Next row With M, cast on 2 sts, P12, turn
and cast on 2 sts.
Work 14 rows in st st and M on these
14 sts only.
Next row [K2 tog] to end.
Next row P1, [P2 tog] to end.
Break off yarn, thread end through rem
sts, pull up and secure. Join seam.
With right side facing, rejoin M yarn to
base of thumb, pick up and K3 sts from
base of thumb, then K last 20 sts of 15th
row of Chart, K first st. 42 sts. Complete
as given for Right Hand from *** to end.

Socks

With 2¾mm (No 12/US 1) needles and M,
cast on 49 sts for cuff.
1st row (right side) K1, [P1, K1] to end.
2nd row P1, [K1, P1] to end.
Rep last 2 rows once more.
Change to 3¼mm (No 10/US 3) needles.
Next row K the 24 sts of 5th row of Chart
twice, then K first st.
Next row P last st of 6th row of Chart,
then P the 24 sts twice.
Work a further 19 rows in patt from Chart
as set.
Cont in M only. Place marker at end of
last row to indicate end of rounds.
Change to set of four 2¾mm (No 12/US 1)
needles. P1 round, dec 7 sts evenly
across. 42 sts. Work 41 rounds in K1, P1
rib.
Change to set of four 3¼mm (No 10/US 3)
needles. Work 4 rounds in st st (every
round K). Break off yarn.
Shape heel
Slip last 9 sts of last round and first 9 sts
of next round onto one needle for heel,
divide rem 24 sts onto 2 needles.
With right side facing, rejoin yarn to 18
heel sts. Work 10 rows in st st on these
sts only.
Next row K13, K2 tog tbl, turn.
Next row Sl 1, P8, P2 tog, turn.
*Next row Sl 1, K8, K2 tog tbl, turn.
Next row Sl 1, P8, P2 tog, turn. *
Rep from * to * twice. 10 sts. Break off
yarn.
Next row Reset sts onto 3 needles as
follows: Slip first 5 sts of heel sts onto a
safety pin, place marker here, rejoin yarn
to rem sts, with first needle K5, then pick
up and K8 sts along side of heel, K5, with
second needle, K14, with third needle,
K5, then pick up and K8 sts along other
side of heel, K5 from safety pin. 50 sts.
K 1 round.
Next round K12, K2 tog, K to last 14 sts,
K2 tog tbl, K12.
K 1 round.
Next round K11, K2 tog, K to last 13 sts,
K2 tog tbl, K11.
K 1 round.
Next round K10, K2 tog, K to last 12 sts,
K2 tog tbl, K10.
Cont in this way, dec 2 sts as set on every
alt row until 40 sts rem.
Cont straight in st st for a further 5cm/2in.
Shape toes
Next round [K7, K2 tog, K2, K2 tog tbl,
K7] twice.
K 1 round.
Next round [K6, K2 tog, K2, K2 tog tbl,
K6] twice.
K 1 round.
Next round [K5, K2 tog, K2, K2 tog tbl,
K5] twice.
Cont in this way, dec 4 sts as set on every
alt round until 20 sts rem.
Divide sts onto 2 needles (sole and
instep) and graft sts.
Join cuff seam. Turn back cuff. Make one
more.

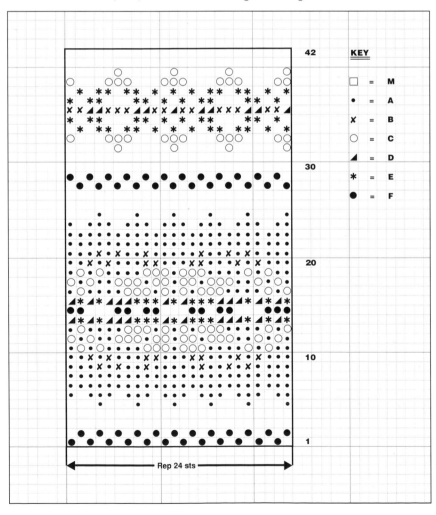

	42	**KEY**
		☐ = M
		• = A
		✕ = B
	30	○ = C
		◢ = D
		* = E
	20	● = F
	10	
	1	

← Rep 24 sts →

Tweedy Hat and Mittens

See Page 34

MATERIALS
2×50g balls of Hayfield Grampian DK in Black (M).
1×50g ball of same in each of Yellow, Green and Red.
Pair each of 3¼mm (No 10/US 3) and 4mm (No 8/US 5) knitting needles.

MEASUREMENTS
To fit age
3–4 years

TENSION
26 sts and 26 rows to 10cm/4in square over pattern on 4mm (No 8/US 5) needles.

ABBREVIATIONS
See page 41.

NOTE
Read Chart from right to left on K rows and from left to right on P rows. Strand yarn not in use loosely across wrong side over no more than 4 sts at a time to keep fabric elastic.

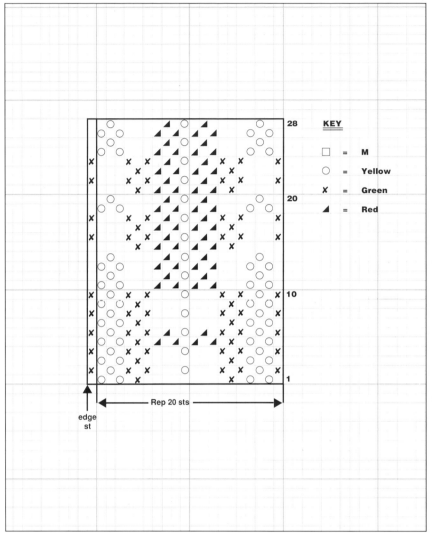

28
20
10
1
← Rep 20 sts →
edge st

KEY
□ = M
○ = Yellow
X = Green
◢ = Red

Hat

With 3¼mm (No 10/US 3) needles and M, cast on 106 sts.
Work 3 rows in K1, P1 rib.
Inc row Rib 3, [inc in next st, rib 6] to last 5 sts, inc in next st, rib 4. 121 sts.
Change to 4mm (No 8/US 5) needles.
Beg with a K row, cont in st st and patt from Chart until work measures 14cm/5½in from beg, ending with a wrong side row.
Shape top
Keeping patt correct, work as follows:
Dec row K1, [sl 1, K1, psso, patt 55, K2 tog, K1] twice.
Dec row P1, [P2 tog, patt 53, P2 tog tbl, P1] twice.
Dec row K1, [sl 1, K1, psso, patt 51, K2 tog, K1] twice.
Dec row P1, [P2 tog, patt 49, P2 tog tbl, P1] twice.
Cont in this way, dec 4 sts as set on every row until 17 sts rem. Break off yarns, thread one end through rem sts, pull up and secure. Join back seam. With Yellow, Green and Red, make pompon and attach to top of hat.
Fold over pointed top to one side and catch down in place.

Mittens

Right Hand
With 3¼mm (No 10/US 3) needles and M, cast on 38 sts.
Work 4cm/1½in in K1, P1 rib, inc 3 sts evenly across last row. 41 sts.
Eyelet hole row K1, [yf, sl 1, K1, psso] to

end. P1 row.
Change to 4mm (No 8/US 5) needles.
Beg with a K row, cont in st st and patt from Chart, work 10 rows. **
Shape for thumb
Next row Patt 21, with M, K6, turn.
Next row With M, cast on 6, P12, turn.
Work in M on these 12 sts only for 4cm/1½in, ending with a P row.
Dec row [K2 tog] to end.
Break off yarn, thread end through rem sts pull up and secure. Join seam.
With right side facing, rejoin M to base of thumb, pick up and K6 sts from base of thumb, then patt rem 14 sts. 41 sts.
***Cont in patt across all sts until work measures 15cm/6in from beg, ending with a wrong side row.
Keeping patt correct, work as follows:
Dec row K1, [sl 1, K1, psso, patt 15, K2 tog, K1] twice.
Patt 1 row.
Dec row K1, [sl 1, K1, psso, patt 13, K2 tog, K1] twice.
Patt 1 row.

Dec row K1, [sl 1, K1, psso, patt 11, K2 tog, K1] twice.
Cast off rem 29 sts. Join seam. Using two strands of M together, make cord approximately 43cm/17in long and thread through eyelet holes. With Yellow, Green and Red, make 2 pompons and attach one to each end of cord.

Left Hand
Work as given for Right Hand to **.
Shape for thumb
Next row Patt 14, with M, K6, turn.
Next row With M, P6, turn and cast on 6 sts.
Work in M on these 12 sts only for 4cm/1½in, ending with a P row.
Dec row [K2 tog] to end.
Break off yarn, thread end through rem sts, pull up and secure. Join seam.
With right side facing, rejoin M to base of thumb, pick up and K6 sts from base of thumb, then patt rem 21 sts. 41 sts.
Complete as given for Right Hand from *** to end.

Diamond Pattern Crochet Hat

See Page 36

MATERIALS
1 × 50g ball of Hayfield Silky Cotton DK in each of 2 colours (A and B). 3.50mm crochet hook.

MEASUREMENTS
To fit age
5–7 years

TENSION
20 dc and 23 rows to 10cm/4in square on 3.50mm hook.

ABBREVIATIONS
Ch = chain; dc = double crochet; 2 dc tog = [insert hook in next dc and draw loop through] twice, yarn over hook and draw through all loops on hook – decrease made; 3 dc tog = [insert hook in next dc and draw loop through] 3 times, yarn over hook and draw through all loops on hook – decrease made.
Also see page 41.

To Make
With 3.50mm hook and A, make 100 ch.
Foundation row 1 dc in 2nd ch from hook, [1 dc in next ch] to end, turn. 99 sts.
Stranding yarn not in use loosely across wrong side over no more than 4 sts at a time and changing colour on the last loop of preceding stitch, work in patt as follows:
1st row (right side) With A, 1 dc in each of first 7 dc, [with B, 1 dc in next dc, with A, 1 dc in each of next 13 dc] 6 times, with B, 1 dc in next dc, with A, 1 dc in each of last 7 dc, turn.
2nd row With A, 1 dc in each of first 6 dc, [with B, 1 dc in each of next 3 dc, with A, 1 dc in each of [next 13 dc] 6 times, with B, 1 dc in next dc, with A, 1 dc in each of next 11 dc] 6 times, with B, 1 dc in each of next 3 dc, with A, 1 dc in each of last 6 dc, turn.
3rd row With A, 1 dc in each of first 5 dc, [with B, 1 dc in each of next 5 dc, with A, 1 dc in each of next 9 dc] 6 times, with B, 1 dc in each of next 5 dc, with A, 1 dc in each of last 5 dc, turn.
4th row With A, 1 dc in each of first 4 dc, [with B, 1 dc in each of next 7 dc, with A, 1 dc in each of next 7 dc] 6 times, with B, 1 dc in each of next 7 dc, with A, 1 dc in each of last 4 dc, turn.
5th row With A, 1 dc in each of first 3 dc, [with B, 1 dc in each of next 9 dc, with A, 1 dc in each of next 5 dc] 6 times, with B, 1 dc in each of next 9 dc, with A, 1 dc in each of last 3 dc, turn.
6th row With A, 1 dc in each of first 2 dc, [with B, 1 dc in each of next 11 dc, with A, 1 dc in each of next 3 dc] 6 times, with B, 1 dc in each of next 11 dc, with A, 1 dc in each of last 2 dc, turn.
7th row With A, 1 dc in first dc, [with B, 1 dc in each of next 13 dc, with A, 1 dc in next dc] 7 times, turn.
8th row As 6th row.
9th row As 5th row.
10th row As 4th row.
11th row As 3rd row.
12th row As 2nd row.
13th row As 1st row.
14th row With A, 1 dc in first dc, [1 dc in next dc] to end, turn.
15th row With B, work as 14th row.
16th row As 14th row.
17th to 24th rows Work 1st to 8th rows.
Shape top
Dec row With A, 2 dc tog, 1 dc in next dc, [with B, 1 dc in each of next 9 dc, with A, 1 dc in next dc, 3 dc tog, 1 dc in next dc] 6 times, with B, 1 dc in each of next 9 dc, with A, 1 dc in next dc, 2 dc tog, turn.
Dec row With A, 2 dc tog, 1 dc in next dc, [with B, 1 dc in each of next 7 dc, with A, 1 dc in next dc, 3 dc tog, 1 dc in next dc] 6 times, with B, 1 dc in each of next 7 dc, with A, 1 dc in next dc, 2 dc tog, turn.
Dec row With A, 2 dc tog, 1 dc in next dc, [with B, 1 dc in each of next 5 dc, with A, 1 dc in next dc, 3 dc tog, 1 dc in next dc] 6 times, with B, 1 dc in each of next 5 dc, with A, 1 dc in next dc, 2 dc tog, turn.
Dec row With A, 2 dc tog, 1 dc in next dc, [with B, 1 dc in each of next 3 dc, with A, 1 dc in next dc, 3 dc tog, 1 dc in next dc] 6 times, with B, 1 dc in each of next 3 dc, with A, 1 dc in next dc, 2 dc tog, turn.
Dec row With A, 2 dc tog, 1 dc in next dc, [with B, 1 dc in next dc, with A, 1 dc in next dc, 3 dc tog, 1 dc in next dc] 6 times, with B, 1 dc in next dc, with A, 1 dc in next dc, 2 dc tog, turn. 29 sts.
Next row With A, 1 dc in first dc, [1 dc in next dc] to end, turn.
Dec row With B, 1 dc in first dc, [2 dc tog] to end, turn.
With A, rep last dec row. Fasten off.
With B and right side facing, work 1 row of dc along lower edge of hat. Fasten off.
Run a gathering thread along top edge pull up and secure. Join seam.

Striped Crochet Hat

See Page 36

MATERIALS
1 × 50g ball of Hayfield Silky Cotton DK in each of 2 colours (A and B). 3.50mm crochet hook.

MEASUREMENTS
To fit age
4–7 years

TENSION
17 sts and 12 rows to 10cm/4in square over pattern on 3.50mm hook.

ABBREVIATIONS
Ch = chain; dc = double crochet; ss = slip stitch; sp = space; tr = treble.
Also see page 41.

To Make
With 3.50mm hook and A, make 6 ch and join into ring with ss.
1st round With A, work 10 dc into ring, ss in first dc.
2nd round With A, 3 ch, 1 tr in first dc (counts as V st), [2 tr in next dc (V st made)] to end, ss in top of 3 ch. Fasten off. 10 V sts.
3rd round Ss B into sp of first V st, 3 ch, 1 tr in sp of first V st, [1 V st in sp of next V st] to end, ss in top of 3 ch. Fasten off.
4th round Ss A in sp of first V st, 3 ch, 1 tr in first V st, 1 V st in first V st, [2 V sts in next V st] to end, ss in top of 3 ch. Fasten off. 20 V sts.
5th round As 3rd round.
6th round Ss A in sp of first V st, 3 ch, 1 tr in first V st, [2 V sts in next V st, 1 V st in next V st] to last V st, 2 V sts in last V st, ss in top of 3 ch. Fasten off. 30 V sts.
7th round As 3rd round.
8th round Ss A in sp of first V st, 3 ch, 1 tr in first V st, [2 V sts in next V st, 1 V st in each of next 2 V sts] to last 2 V sts, 2 V sts in next V st, 1 V st in last V st, ss in top of 3 ch. Fasten off. 40 V sts.
9th round As 3rd round.
10th round Ss A in sp of first V st, 3 ch, 1 tr in first V st, [2 V sts in next V st, 1 V st in each of next 7 V sts] to last 7 V sts, 2 V sts in next V st, 1 V st in each of last 6 V sts, ss in top of 3 ch. Fasten off. 45 V sts.
11th round As 3rd round.
12th round With A, work as 3rd round.
Rep last 2 rounds 4 times more.
Next round Ss A in sp of first V st, 1 dc in first V st, [3 ch, 1 dc in first of 3 ch (picot made), 1 dc in next V st] to end, 3 ch, 1 dc in first of 3 ch, ss in first dc.
Fasten off.

Striped Beret, Scarf and Gloves

See Page 35

MATERIALS
2×50g balls of Hayfield Pure Wool Classics DK in each of Navy (A) and Red (B).
1×50g ball of same in each of Green (C), Yellow (D) and Cream (E).
Pair of 3¾mm (No 9/US 4) and 4mm (No 8/US 5) knitting needles.
One 4mm (No 8/US 5) circular needle for scarf.

MEASUREMENTS
To fit age
    4–7 years

TENSION
22 sts and 28 rows to 10cm/4in square over reverse st st on 4mm (No 8/US 5) needles.

ABBREVIATIONS
See page 41.

Beret

With 3¾mm (No 9/US 4) needles and A, cast on 89 sts. K 2 rows A, K 2 rows D, K 2 rows C, K 2 rows B and K 2 rows E.
Change to 4mm (No 8/US 5) needles.
K 1 row A.
Inc row (wrong side) K1, [m1, K8] to end. 100 sts.
Beg with a P row and working in reverse st st throughout, cont as follows: Work 3 rows A.
Inc row With A, K1, [m1, K10, m1, K1] to end.
Work 3 rows C.
Inc row With C, K1, [m1, K12, m1, K1] to end.
Work 1 row B, 1 row C and 1 row A.
Inc row With A, K1, [m1, K14, m1, K1] to end.
Work 2 rows A, 1 row E, 1 row A and 1 row B.
Inc row With B, K1, [m1, K16, m1, K1] to end. 172 sts.
Work 2 rows B, 1 row D, 1 row A and 4 rows B.
Shape top
Dec row With A, [P15, P2 tog] to last 2 sts, P2.
Work 1 row A.
Dec row With A, [P14, P2 tog] to last 2 sts, P2.
Work 1 row A.
Dec row With A, [P13, P2 tog] to last 2 sts, P2.
Working stripes of 6 rows E, 1 row B, 3 rows E, 4 rows C, 1 row D, 2 rows C, 3 rows B, 1 row A, 2 rows D and 1 row A, **at the same time**, dec 10 sts as set on every alt row until 22 sts rem. Work 1 row A.
Dec row With A, [P2 tog] to end.
Break off yarn, thread end through rem sts, pull up and secure. Join seam. Make a large pompon with all colours and attach to top of beret.

Scarf

With 4mm (No 8/US 5) circular needle and A, cast on 212 sts.
Work backwards and forwards as follows:
K 2 rows A, K 2 rows D, K 2 rows C, K 2 rows B, K 2 rows E and K 1 row A.

Inc row (wrong side) With A, K8, [K twice in next st, K14] to last 9 sts, K twice in next st, K8. 226 sts.
Beg with a P row, work in reverse st st and stripes of 4 rows A, 4 rows C, 1 row B, 1 row C, 4 rows A, 1 row E, 1 row A, 4 rows B, 1 row D, 1 row A, 4 rows B, 1 row A, 1 row E, 4 rows A, 1 row C, 1 row B, 4 rows C and 5 rows A.
Dec row With A, K8, [K2 tog, K14] to last 10 sts, K2 tog, K8. 212 sts.
K 2 rows E, K 2 rows B, K 2 rows C, K 2 rows D, K 1 row A. With A, cast off knitwise.
Cut yarns into 25cm/10in lengths and using 3 strands together, fringe each end of scarf with colours according to stripes. Trim fringe.

Gloves

With 3¾mm (No 9/US 4) needles and A, cast on 35 sts. K 2 rows A, K 2 rows D, K 2 rows C, K 2 rows B and K 2 rows E.
Change to 4mm (No 8/US 5) needles.
K 2 rows A. Beg with a P row and working in reverse st st throughout, work 4 rows A.
Shape for thumb
Use separate lengths of yarn for each side of thumb and A for thumb, twisting yarns together on wrong side at joins to avoid holes.
1st row P17C, with A, P twice in next st, P17C.
2nd row K17C, 2A, 17C.
3rd row P17C, with A, P twice in each of next 2 sts, P17C.
4th row K17C, 4A, 17C.
5th row P17B, with A, P twice in next st, P2, P twice in next st, P17B.
6th row K17C, 6A, 17C.
7th row With A, P17, P twice in next st, P4, P twice in next st, P17.
8th row With A, K.
9th row With A, P17, P twice in next st, P6, P twice in next st, P17.
10th row With A, K.
11th row P17E, with A, P twice in next st, P8, P twice in next st, P17E. 46 sts.
12th row With A, K.
Next row P17B, 12A, turn.
Next row With A, cast on 1 st, K13, turn and cast on 1 st.
With A, work 10 rows on these 14 sts

only.
Dec row P2 tog, [P1, P2 tog] to end.
K 1 row.
Dec row [P1, P2 tog] to end. 6 sts.
Break off yarn, thread end through rem sts, pull up and secure. Join seam.
With right side facing and B, pick up and K2 sts from base of thumb, P rem 17 sts. 36 sts. Work 2 rows B, 1 row D, 1 row A, 3 rows B and 2 rows A.
Shape for fingers
Next row P4E, 4C, 5D, 10B, turn.
Next row With B, cast on 1 st, K11, turn and cast on 1 st.
With B, work 16 rows on these 12 sts only for first finger.
Dec row [P1, P2 tog] to end.
K 1 row.
Dec row P2 tog, [P1, P2 tog] to end. 5 sts.
Break off yarn, thread end through rem sts, pull up and secure. Join seam.
With right side facing and D, pick up and K2 sts from base of first finger, P5, turn.
Next row With D, cast on 1 st, K6, K2 tog, K5, turn and cast on 1 st.
With D, work 18 rows on these 13 sts only for second finger.
Dec row P1, [P2 tog, P1] to end.
K 1 row.
Dec row [P1, P2 tog] to end. 6 sts.
Break off yarn, thread end through rem sts, pull up and secure. Join seam.
With right side facing and C, pick up and K2 sts from base of second finger, P4, turn.
Next row With C, cast on 1 st, K11, turn and cast on 1 st.
With C, work 16 rows on these 12 sts only for third finger Complete as given for first finger.
With right side facing and E, pick up and K2 sts from base of third finger, P4. With E, work 11 rows on rem 10 sts for fourth finger.
Dec row P1, [P2 tog, P1] to end.
K 1 row.
Dec row P1, [P2 tog, P1] to end. 5 sts.
Break off yarn, thread end through rem sts, pull up and secure. Join finger and side seam. Make one more.

Fair Isle Beret and Gloves

See Page
37

MATERIALS
2×50g balls of Hayfield Pure Wool Classics DK in Natural (MC).
Small amount of same in each of Light Blue (A), Dark Blue (B), Light Yellow (C), Dark Yellow (D), Navy (E), Red (F) and Pink (G).
Pair each of 3¼mm (No 10/US 3), 3¾mm (No 9/US 4) and 4mm (No 8/US 5) knitting needles.

MEASUREMENTS
To fit age
5–7 years

TENSION
22 sts and 28 rows to 10cm/4in square over st st on 4mm (No 8/US 5) needles.

ABBREVIATIONS
See page 41.

NOTE
Read Chart from right to left on K rows and from left to right on P rows. When working in pattern, strand yarn not in use loosely across wrong side over no more than 4 sts at a time to keep fabric elastic.

Beret

With 3¼mm (No 10/US 3) needles and MC, cast on 92 sts. Work 7 rows in K1, P1 rib.
Inc row Rib 6, [m1, rib 2] to last 4 sts, rib 4. 133 sts.
Change to 4mm (No 8/US 5) needles.
Beg with a K row and working in st st throughout, work 2 rows.
Next row 1MC, [1E, 1MC] to end.
Next row 1E, [1MC, 1E] to end.
Work 1 row MC.
Inc row With MC, P3, [m1, P5] to end. 159 sts.
Work patt as follows:
1st row 2MC, [1F, 1MC, 1F, 5MC] to last 5 sts, 1F, 1MC, 1F, 2MC.
2nd row 1MC, [2F, 1MC, 2F, 3MC] to last 6 sts, 2F, 1MC, 1MC.
3rd row 3MC, [1G, 3MC] to end.
4th row As 2nd row.
5th row As 1st row.
Work 1 row MC.
Inc row With MC, K1, m1, K4, m1, [K7, m1] to last 7 sts, K6, m1, K1. 183 sts.
Now work 1st to 19th rows of Chart.
Shape top
Dec row With A, K1, * [K2 tog] 3 times, K1, [K2 tog] 4 times, [K1, K2 tog] twice, [K2 tog] twice, K1; rep from * to end. 106 sts.
Next row With A, P to last 2 sts, P2 tog.
Next row 1A, [1E, 1A] to end.
Next row 1E, [1MC, 1E] to end.
Work 2 rows MC.
Dec row With MC, K1, K2 tog, *[K1F,

1MC] twice, with MC, [K2 tog] 4 times; rep from * to last 6 sts, K1F, 1MC, 1F, with MC, K2 tog, K1. 71 sts.
Now work 2nd to 5th rows of patt, then work 1 row MC.
Dec row With MC, K1, * [K2 tog, K1] twice, K2 tog; rep from * to last 6 sts, [K2 tog, K1] twice. 45 sts.
Next row 1E, [1MC, 1E] to end.
Next row 1A, [1E, 1A] to end.
Work 3 rows A.
Dec row With A, K1, [K2 tog] to end. P 1 row A.
Dec row With A, K1, [K2 tog] to end. 12 sts.
Break off yarn, thread end through rem sts, pull up and secure. Join seam.

Gloves

Right hand
With 3¼mm (No 10/US 3) needles and MC, cast on 36 sts.
Work 4cm/1½in in K1, P1 rib.
Inc row Rib 2, [inc in next st, rib 5] to last 4 sts, inc in next st, rib 3. 42 sts.
Change to 4mm (No 8/US 5) needles.
Beg with a K row and working in st st throughout, work 2 rows.
Work patt from Chart as follows:
1st row (right side) Work 4th to 24th sts of the 26 sts of 1st row of Chart twice.
2nd row Work 24th to 4th sts of the 26 sts of 2nd row of Chart twice.
Cont working from Chart as set, work a further 10 rows. **
Shape for thumb
Next row Patt 22, with MC, K7, turn.
Change to 3¾mm (No 9/US 4) needles.
Next row With MC, P7, turn and cast on 6 sts.
*** Work in MC on these 13 sts only for 14 rows.
Dec row K1, [K2 tog] to end.
P1 row. Break off yarn, thread end through rem sts, pull up and secure.
Join seam.
With right side facing, 4mm (No 8/US 5) needles and colours as required by patt, pick up and K7 sts from base of thumb, patt to end. 42 sts.

Work a further 6 rows in patt, then work 1 row A.
Dec row With A, [K4, K2 tog, K5, K2 tog] 3 times, K3. 36 sts.
Next row [P1E, 1A] to end.
Next row [K1E, 1MC] to end.
Change to 3¾mm (No 9/US 4) needles.
Cont in MC only, work 1 row.
Shape for fingers
Next row K23, turn.
Next row Cast on 1 st, P11, turn and cast on 1 st.
Work 16 rows on these 12 sts only for first finger.
Dec row [K2 tog] to end.
P 1 row. Break off yarn, thread end through rem sts, pull up and secure.
Join seam.
With right side facing, rejoin yarn to base of first finger, pick up and K2 sts from base of first finger, K5, turn.
Next row Cast on 1 st, P13, turn and cast on 1 st.
Work 18 rows on these 14 sts only for second finger. Complete as given for first finger.
With right side facing, rejoin yarn to base of second finger, pick up and K2 sts from base of second finger, K4, turn.
Next row Cast on 1 st, P11, turn and cast on 1 st.
Work 16 rows on these 12 sts only for third finger. Complete as given for first finger.
With right side facing, rejoin yarn to base of third finger, pick up and K3 sts from base of third finger, K rem 4 sts. Work 11 rows on rem 11 sts for fourth finger.
Dec row K1, [K2 tog] to end.
P 1 row. Break off yarn, thread end through rem sts, pull up and secure.
Join finger and side seam.

Left hand
Work as given for Right Hand to **.
Shape for thumb
Next row Patt 13, with MC, K7, turn.
Change to 3¾mm (No 9/US 4) needles.
Next row With MC, cast on 6 sts, P13, turn.
Complete as given for Right Hand from *** to end.

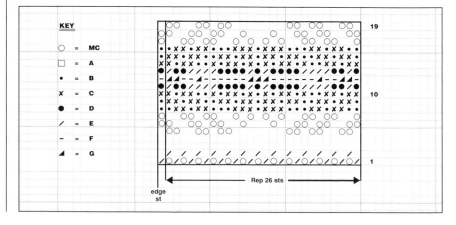

"Birds" Hat and Bag

See Page
38

MATERIALS
1 × 50g ball of Hayfield Silky Cotton DK in each of Burgundy (A), Purple (B) and Navy (C).
Small amount of same in each of Yellow, Orange, Green, Red and Lilac.
Pair each of 3¼mm (No 10/US 3) and 3¾mm (No 9/US 4) knitting needles.
Medium-size crochet hook.

MEASUREMENTS
To fit age
5–7 years

TENSION
24 sts and 30 rows to 10cm/4in square over st st on 3¾mm (No 9/US 4) needles.

ABBREVIATIONS
See page 41.

NOTE
Read Chart from right to left on K rows and from left to right on P rows. When working in pattern, use separate lengths of yarn for each coloured area and twist yarns together on wrong side at joins to avoid holes.

Hat

With 3¼mm (No 10/US 3) needles and A, cast on 121 sts.
Beg with a K row, work 5 rows in st st. K1 row for foldline.
Change to 3¾mm (No 9/US 4) needles.
Beg with a K row, work in st st and patt from Chart until 37th row of Chart has been worked. Cont in A only, K 1 row.
Beg with a K row, work 4 rows in st st.
Next (tuck) row [K next st tog with corresponding st 9 rows below (34th row of patt)] to end.
P 1 row.
Shape top
Dec row [K13 , K2 tog] to last st, K1.
P 1 row.
Dec row [K12, K2 tog] to last st, K1.
P 1 row.
Dec row [K11, K2 tog] to last st, K1.
Cont in this way, dec 8 sts as set on every alt row until 25 sts rem. P 1 row.
Dec row [K2 tog] to last st, K1.
Break off yarn, thread end through rem sts, pull up and secure.
Work 1 row of stem stitch between A and B bands of pattern with Red and between B and C bands with Lilac. With Yellow and stem stitch, outline birds and work French knot for eyes. Join seam. Fold hem to wrong side at foldline and slip stitch in place.

Bag

Begin at lower edge.
With 3¼mm (No 10/US 3) needles and A, cast on 61 sts.
Beg with a K row, work 5 rows in st st. K 1 row.
Change to 3¾mm (No 9/US 4) needles.
Beg with a K row, work in st st and patt from Chart, work 1st to 33rd rows once, then work 1st to 37th rows. Cont in A only, K 2 rows. Beg with a K row, work 5 rows in st st. Cast off purlwise.
Work 1 row of stem stitch between all A and B bands of pattern with Red, between all B and C bands with Lilac and between all C and A bands with Orange. With Yellow and stem stitch, outline birds and work French knot for eyes.
Make one more.
Join side and lower edge seams. Fold last 5 rows of st st to wrong side and slip stitch in place.
With 3¼mm (No 10/US 3) needles and A, cast on 6 sts for strap. Work in garter st (every row K) until strap measures approximately 71cm/28in. Cast off knitwise. Sew ends to wrong side at side seams. With crochet hook and A, make a chain cord approximately 100cm/39¼in long. Thread through sts along folded st st hem on wrong side. With A, make 2 tassels and attach one to each end of cord.

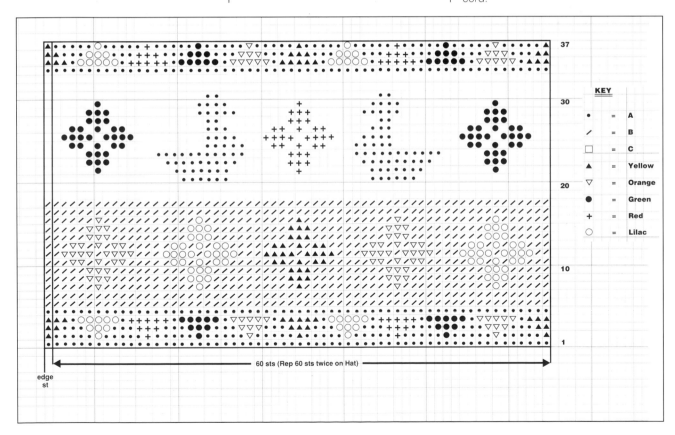

60 sts (Rep 60 sts twice on Hat)

edge st

KEY

•	=	A
╱	=	B
□	=	C
▲	=	Yellow
▽	=	Orange
●	=	Green
+	=	Red
○	=	Lilac

Two-colour Beret, Gloves and Socks

See Page
39

MATERIALS
2 × 50g balls of Hayfield Grampian DK in each of 2 colours (A and B).
Pair of 3¼mm (No 10/US 3), 3¾mm (No 9/US 4) and 4mm (No 8/US 5) knitting needles.
Set of four 4mm (No 8/US 5) double-pointed knitting needles for socks.

MEASUREMENTS
To fit age
 4 – 6 years

TENSION
22 sts and 28 rows to 10 cm/4in square over st st on 4mm (No 8/US 5) needles.

ABBREVIATIONS
See page 41.

NOTE
When working in pattern, use separate small balls of yarn for each coloured area and twist yarns together on wrong sides at joins to avoid holes.

Beret

With 3¾mm (No 9/US 4) needles and A, cast on 85 sts. K 14 rows.
Inc row [P1, m1] twice, [P2, m1] to last 3 sts, [P1, m1] twice, P1. 129 sts.
Change to 4mm (No 8/US 5) needles.
Beg with a K row and working in st st throughout, work in patt as follows:
1st and 2nd rows 1A, [15B, 1A] to end.
3rd and 4th rows 2A, [13B, 3A] to last 15 sts, 13B, 2A.
5th (inc) row 1A, [with A, m1, 2A, 11B, 2A, with A, m1, 1A] to end. 145 sts.
6th row 4A, [11B, 7A] to last 15 sts, 11B, 4A.
7th and 8th rows 5A, [9B, 9A] to last 14 sts, 9B, 5A.
9th and 10th rows 6A, [7B, 11A] to last 13 sts, 7B, 6A.
11th (inc) row 1A, [with A, m1, 6A, 5B, 6A, with A, m1, 1A] to end. 161 sts.
12th row 8A, [5B, 15A] to last 13 sts, 5B, 8A.
13th and 14th rows 9A, [3B, 17A] to last 12 sts, 3B, 9A.
15th and 16th rows 10A, [1B, 19A] to last 11 sts, 1B, 10A.
Cont in A only, work 8 rows.
Shape top
Dec row [K14, K2 tog] to last st, K1.
P 1 row.
Dec row [K13, K2 tog] to last st, K1.
P 1 row.
Dec row [K12, K2 tog] to last st, K1.

Cont in this way, dec 10 sts as set on every alt row until 21 sts rem.
P 1 row.
Dec row [K2 tog] to last st, K1.
Break off yarn, thread end through rem sts, pull up and secure. Join seam.

Gloves

With 3¾mm (No 9/US 4) needles and B, cast on 35 sts. K 4 rows.
Change to 4mm (No 8/US 5) needles.
Beg with a K row and working in st st throughout, work 2 rows.
Work in patt as follows:
1st and 2nd rows 17B, 1A, 17B.
3rd and 4th rows 1A, 15B, 3A, 15B, 1A.
5th and 6th rows 2A, 13B, 5A, 13B, 2A.
7th and 8th rows 3A, 11B, 7A, 11B, 3A.
Shape for thumb
9th (inc) row 4A, 9B, 4A, with A, m1, 1A, with A, m1, 4A, 9B, 4A.
10th row 4A, 9B, 11A, 9B, 4A.
11th (inc) row 5A, 7B, 5A, with A, m1, 3A, with A, m1, 5A, 7B, 5A.
12th row 5A, 7B, 15A, 7B, 5A.
13th (inc) row 6A, 5B, 6A, with A, m1, 5A, with A, m1, 6A, 5B, 6A.
14th row 6A, 5B, 19A, 5B, 6A.
15th (inc) row 7A, 3B, 7A, [with A, m1, 7A] twice, 3B, 7A.
16th row 7A, 3B, 23A, 3B, 7A.
17th (inc) row 8A, 1B, 8A, with A, m1, 9A, with A, m1, 8A, 1B, 8A.
18th row 8A, 1B, 27A, 1B, 8A. 45 sts.
Cont in A only.
Next row K28, turn.
Next row Cast on 1 st, P12, turn and cast on 1 st.
Work 8 rows on these 13 sts only.
Dec row K1, [K2 tog, K1] 4 times.
P 1 row.
Dec row [K1, K2 tog] 3 times.
Break off yarn, thread end through rem sts, pull up and secure. Join seam.
With right side facing, rejoin yarn to base of thumb, pick up and K2 sts from base of thumb, K rem 17 sts. 36 sts. Work 9 rows across all sts.
Shape for fingers
Next row K23, turn.
Next row Cast on 1 st, P11, turn and cast on 1 st.
Work 14 rows on these 12 sts only for first finger.
Dec row [K1, K2 tog] 4 times.
P 1 row.
Dec row K2 tog, [K1, K2 tog] twice.
Break off yarn, thread end through rem sts, pull up and secure. Join seam.
With right side facing, rejoin yarn to base of first finger, pick up and K1 st from base of first finger, K5, turn.
Next row Cast on 1 st, P12, turn and cast on 1 st.

Work 16 rows on these 13 sts only for second finger. Complete as given for thumb.
With right side facing, rejoin yarn to base of second finger, pick up and K2 sts from base of second finger, K4, turn.
Next row Cast on 1 st, P11, turn and cast on 1 st.
Complete third finger as given for first finger.
With right side facing, rejoin yarn to base of third finger, pick up and K2 sts from base of third finger, K rem 4 sts.
Work 9 rows on rem 10 sts for fourth finger.
Dec row K1, [K2 tog, K1] 3 times.
P1 row.
Dec row K1, [K2 tog, K1] twice.
Break off yarn, thread end through rem sts, pull up and secure. Join finger and side seam.
Make one more.

Socks

With 3¼mm (No 10/US 3) needles and A, cast on 37 sts.
1st row (right side) K1, [P1, K1] to end.
2nd row P1, [K1, P1] to end.
Rep last 2 rows 4 times more.
Change to 4mm (No 8/US 5) needles.
Beg with a K row and working in st st throughout, work 4 rows.
Work in patt as follows:
1st and 2nd rows 9A, 1B, 17A, 1B, 9A.
3rd and 4th rows 8A, 3B, 15A, 3B, 8A.
5th and 6th rows 7A, 5B, 13A, 5B, 7A.
7th and 8th rows 6A, 7B, 11A, 7B, 6A.
9th and 10th rows 5A, 9B, 9A, 9B, 5A.
11th and 12th rows 4A, 11B, 7A, 11B, 4A.
13th and 14th rows 3A, 13B, 5A, 13B, 3A.
15th and 16th rows 2A, 15B, 3A, 15B, 2A.
17th and 18th rows 1A, [17B, 1A] twice.
Break off yarns.
Reset sts onto 3 of the set of four 4mm (No 8/US 5) double-pointed needles as follows: slip first 9 sts onto one needle, slip next 10 sts onto second needle and next 9 sts onto third needle, slip last 9 sts onto other end of first needle. With right side facing, rejoin B to sts on first needle and work 7 rounds of st st (every round K). Cont in B only.
Shape heel
Next row K18, turn.
Next row P18, turn.
Work 10 rows on these 18 sts only.
Dec row K13, sl 1, K1, psso, turn.
Dec row Sl 1, P8, P2 tog, turn.
Dec row Sl 1, K8, sl 1, K1, psso, turn.
Dec row Sl 1, K8, sl 1, K1, psso, turn.
Dec row Sl 1, P8, P2 tog, turn.

Rep last 2 rows twice more. 10 sts. Break off yarn.
Reset sts onto 3 double-pointed needles as follows: slip first 5 heel sts onto safety pin, place marker here to indicate ends of rounds, rejoin yarn and with first needle, K rem 5 heel sts, pick up and K9 sts up side edge of heel, K3, with second needle, K13, with third needle, K3, then pick up and K9 sts up other side edge of heel, K5 sts from safety pin. 47 sts. K 1 round.
Dec round K13, K2 tog, K to last 15 sts, sl 1, K1, psso, K13.

K 1 round.
Dec round K12, K2 tog, K to last 14 sts, sl 1, K1, psso, K12.
K 1 round.
Dec round K11, K2 tog, K to last 13 sts, sl 1, K1, psso, K11.
Cont in this way, dec 2 sts as set on every alt round until 37 sts rem.
K 20 rounds.
Shape toes
Dec round K6, K2 tog, K2, sl 1, K1, psso, K13, K2 tog, K10.
K 1 round.

Dec round [K5, K2 tog, K2, sl 1, K1, psso, K6] twice.
K 1 round.
Dec round [K4, K2 tog, K2, sl 1, K1, psso, K5] twice.
K1 round.
Dec round [K3, K2 tog, K2, sl 1, K1, psso, K4] twice.
Cont in this way, dec 4 sts as set on every alt round until 14 sts rem.
K 1 round. Divide sts onto 2 needles (sole and instep) and graft sts.
Join seam. Make one more.

Fair Isle Ski Hat and Generous Mittens

See Page
40

MATERIALS
2×50g balls of Hayfield Grampian DK in Black (M).
1×50g ball of same in each of Green (A), Turquoise (B) and Pink (C).
Small amount of same in each of Yellow (D) and Red (E).
Pair each of 3¾mm (No 9/US 4) and 4mm (No 8/US 5) knitting needles.

MEASUREMENTS
To fit age
3–7 years

TENSION
24 sts and 25 rows to 10cm/4in square over pattern on 4mm (No 8/US 5) needles.

ABBREVIATIONS
See page 41.

NOTE
Read Charts from right to left on K rows and from left to right on P rows. When working pattern, strand yarn not in use loosely across wrong side over no more than 4 sts at a time to keep fabric elastic.

Hat

With 4mm (No 8/US 5) needles and M, cast on 113 sts.
1st row K1, [P1, K1] to end.
2nd row P1, [K1, P1] to end.
Beg with a K row, work in st st and brim patt from Chart 1 until 14th row of Chart 1 has been worked. With M, K1 row.
Dec row K6, [K2 tog, K9] to last 8 sts, K2 tog, K6. 103 sts.
Beg with a P row, work 24 rows in st st.
Inc row P6, [inc in next st, P9] to last 7 sts, inc in next st, P6. 113 sts.
Cont in st st, work 1st to 21st rows of Chart 2, then 1st to 18th rows of Chart 3.
Shape top
Dec row With M, P2, P2 tog, P3, * P2 tog,

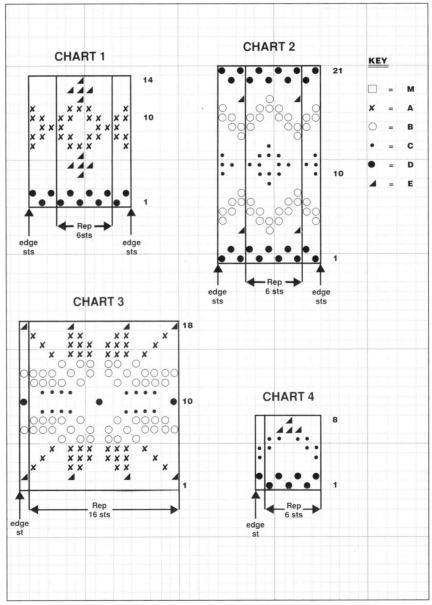

continued overleaf

P4, [P2 tog P3] twice; rep from * to last 10 sts, P2 tog, P3, P2 tog, P1. 91 sts.
Now work 1st to 8th rows of Chart 4.
Dec row With M, K1, [K2 tog, K1] to end. 61 sts.
Next row P1M, [1D, 1M] to end.
Next row K1D, [1M, 1D] to end.
P 1 row M.
Dec row K5M, [1B, with M, K1, K2 tog, K1, K2 tog, K1] to end.
Next row P4M, [3B, 3M] to last st, 1M.
Dec row With M, K1, K2 tog, [K2B, 1M] to last 2 sts, with M, K2 tog. 47 sts.
Next row P3M, [3B, 3M] to end.
Next row K4M, [1B, 5M] to last 5 sts, 1B, 4M.
Cont in M only.
Dec row P2, [P2 tog, P1] to last st, P1. P 1 row.
Dec row P1, [P2 tog] to end. 16 sts.
Break off yarn, thread end through rem sts, pull up and secure. Join seam, reversing seam on brim. Turn back brim.

Generous Mittens

Right Hand
With 3¾mm (No 9/US 4) needles and M, cast on 41 sts. K 4 rows.
Change 4mm (No 8/US 5) needles. K 1 row.
Inc row P5, [m1, P6] to end. 47 sts.
Beg with a K row and working in st st throughout, work patt from Chart 2 until 21st row of Chart 2 has been worked. **
Shape for thumb
Next row With M, P24, turn.
Next row With M, cast on 7 sts, K14, turn.
*** With M, work 13 rows on these 14 sts only.
Dec row [K2 tog] to end.
P 1 row.
Dec row K1, [K2 tog] to end. 4 sts.
Break off yarn, thread end through rem sts, pull up and secure. Join seam. With wrong side facing, rejoin M to base of thumb, pick up and P6 sts from base of thumb, P to end. 46 sts.
Work from Chart 3 as follows:
1st row [Work last 4 sts of the 16 sts of 2nd row of Chart 3, rep the 16 sts once, then work first 3 sts of the 16 sts] twice.
2nd row [Work last 3 sts of the 16 sts of 3rd row of Chart 3, rep the 16 sts once, then work first 4 sts of the 16 sts] twice.
Cont working from Chart 3 as set until 18th row of Chart 3 has been worked.
Dec row With M, P1, P2 tog tbl, [P19, P2 tog] twice, P1. 43 sts.
Now work patt from Chart 4, work 2 rows.
Dec row K1, [sl 1, K1, psso, patt 16, K2 tog, K1] twice.
Patt 1 row.
Dec row K1, [sl 1, K1, psso, patt 14, K2 tog, K1] twice.
Patt 1 row.
Dec row K1, [sl 1, K1, psso, patt 12, K2 tog, K1] twice.
Patt 1 row. With M, cast off. Join seam.

Left Hand
Work as given for Right Hand to **.
Shape for thumb
Next row With M, P30, turn.
Next row With M, K, turn and cast on 7 sts.
Complete as given for Right Hand from *** to end.

Source Guide

For local stockists of Hayfield Yarns in your country, please write to the address below:

AUSTRALIA
Panda Yarns (International) Pty Ltd
314–320 Albert Street, West Brunswick, Victoria 3057.
Tel: (03) 387 4033

CANADA
Estelle Designs & Sales Ltd
Unit 65 & 67, 2220 Midland Avenue, Scarborough, Ontario, M1P 3E6.
Tel: (416) 298 9922

DENMARK
Ove Andersen
Harkaor 32, DK–2730, Herlev.
Tel: (42) 910 074

EGYPT
Bahnasy for Trade
5 El Nasr Street, El Khamisi, Alexandria.
Tel: 203 809 409

GERMANY
Geschwister Diehl GMBH
Strahlenderger Strasse 129, 6050 Offenbach.
Tel: 069 829 0080

GREAT BRITAIN
Hayfield Textiles Ltd
Hayfield Mills, Glusburn, Keighley, West Yorkshire BD20 8QP.
Tel: (0535) 633 333

HONG KONG
B P Trading Company
Block G, 9th Floor, Hop Hing Industrial Bldg, 702 Castle Peak Road, Kowloon.
Tel: 741 6268

ICELAND
Arval
PO Box 4011, 124 Reykjavik.
Tel: (1) 687 950

JAPAN
Dia Keito Co Ltd
2–3–11 Senba Higashi, Minho City, Osaka 562.
Tel: 0727 276604

KOREA
Kossell International Inc
CPO Box 9831, Seoul.
Tel: (2) 980 0774

MALAYSIA
Malayan Shoes Machinery SDN BHD
128 Jalan Selar, Taman Bukit Ria, Off Batu 4, Jalan Cheras, 56100 Kuala Lumpur.
Tel: (3) 971 6418

NEW ZEALAND
Katex Enterprises Ltd
Unit 2, Mt Wellington Industrial Park, Allright Place, PO Box 62–2000, Mt Wellington, Auckland.
Tel: (09) 527 3241

NORWAY
Garnglede AS
Sporveisgaten 31, 0354 Oslo 3.
Tel: (2) 606 995

SINGAPORE
Malayan Traders Syndicate Ltd
Maxwell Road, PO Box 929, Singapore 9018.
Tel: 746 6141

SOUTH AFRICA
Paxem Pty Ltd
PO Box 1381, 202 Fanora House, 61 Rissik Street, Johannesburg 2001.
Tel: 011 818 7771

SWEDEN
Svenska Novita
Angdalev 30E, 23634 Hollviken.
Tel: 040 45 3363

UNITED STATES OF AMERICA
Cascade Yarns Inc
204 Third Avenue, South Seattle, Washington 98104.
Tel: (206) 628 2960